# MUSICALS
## —— ON THE ——
# SILVER SCREEN

# MUSICALS
## ── ON THE ──
# SILVER SCREEN

### LEONARD KNIFFEL

an imprint of the American Library Association

HURON STREET PRESS

CHICAGO • 2013

**LEONARD KNIFFEL** is a writer and librarian living in Chicago. He was editor and publisher of *American Libraries*, the magazine of the American Library Association, from 1996 to 2012. A lifelong fan of movie musicals, he is also the author of *Reading with the Stars: A Celebration of Books and Libraries* (American Library Association and Skyhorse Publishing, 2011) and *A Polish Son in the Motherland: An American's Journey Home* (Texas A&M University Press, 2005), a travel memoir.

Published by Huron Street Press, an imprint of ALA Publishing
Printed in the United States of America
17  16  15  14  13      5  4  3  2  1

Extensive effort has gone into ensuring the reliability of the information in this book; however, the publisher makes no warranty, express or implied, with respect to the material contained herein.

ISBNs: 978-1-937589-30-1 (paper); 978-1-937589-48-6 (PDF). For more information on digital formats, visit the ALA Store at alastore.ala.org and select eEditions.

**Library of Congress Cataloging-in-Publication Data**

Kniffel, Leonard.
　　Musicals on the silver screen / Leonard Kniffel.
　　　pages   cm
　　Includes bibliographical references and index.
　　ISBN 978-1-937589-30-1 (alk. paper)
　　1. Musical films—United States—History and criticism.  I. Title.
　　PN1995.9.M86K56 2013
　791.43'6—dc23                                    2013005832

Book design in Miller Text and Brandon Grotesque by Kimberly Thornton

*In memory of my godmother,*
*Helen Gutt Brodacki Riley, and her*
*beautiful voice*

# CONTENTS

# FOREWORD

**WHEN I FIRST STARTED WRITING MUSICALS IN THE LATE 1980S, THE** Internet was in its infancy. You couldn't stream a video, let alone find clips of your favorite musicals on YouTube, which wouldn't come into existence for more than a decade. At that time, for inspiration and to feed my insatiable musical theater addiction, I used to borrow films of classic musicals from the Chicago Public Library, if it had them, or from Facets Multimedia, an art film cinema-bibliothèque in Lincoln Park, just around the corner from my apartment at the time. To this day, I remember the thrill of seeing for the first time the hallucinogenic choreography of "I Only Have Eyes for You" in Busby Berkeley's film *Dames*. Eureka! Suddenly I had discovered what the American musical was all about—a lot of song, a little sap, and a big dose of tap.

Had I had then a copy of Leonard Kniffel's book *Musicals on the Silver Screen*, I would have been in serious danger—danger of never leaving my apartment. Kniffel's book is an invaluable resource and, ironically, much as it would have come in handy to me back in the '80s, it's even more timely now. With the advent of Amazon.com, online streaming video, and YouTube, it's a lot easier to find some of the rare and arcane gems that Kniffel discusses in his book.

*Musicals on the Silver Screen* is nothing short of encyclopedic in its scope. And unlike most invaluable reference books, it's downright entertaining.

Beginning with the first talkie, *The Jazz Singer* (1927), Kniffel takes us on a chronological odyssey that ends, appropriately, with 2011's *The Artist*. Within the scope of those eighty-four years, Kniffel brings us all the important (and, he's the first to admit, some not-so-important) musicals of the decade.

His commentaries on each film are necessarily short, but they contain all the vital information. They are replete with his smart takes on the changing social attitudes of the films as well as being larded with fascinating stories of the stars themselves. Here's Kniffel's perceptive insight on *The Jazz Singer*: "It's ironic that the first sound musical featured a white Jew imitating African American performance style for a primarily WASP audience." Often he interjects an interesting tidbit of cinematic lore, such as how the "silver screen" got its name. I'm not going to tell you that—you'll have to read the book to find out.

It's hard to imagine what fell through the floorboards in *Musicals on the Silver Screen*. The sheer number of films discussed—which Kniffel has viewed and gives thumbnail reviews of—is gargantuan.

As far as I can make out, there's only one thing wrong with this book—it doesn't come with a large bucket of popcorn.

*—Gregg Opelka*

# LEARNING GUIDE

## MOVIE MUSICALS AND THEIR STARS

**MY LOVE AFFAIR WITH MOVIE MUSICALS BEGAN WHEN I WAS ELEVEN** years old. That's when we got our first television. On school days I would sneak out of bed to watch movies late into the night. On weekends I could hardly wait for *Saturday Night at the Movies,* hoping the television premiere that week would be a musical. You could not borrow movies from the public library in those days, nor could you buy them or download them for your home library.

When movies began to talk in 1927, my mother was eight years old and would not enter a movie theater for another ten years. This may explain why at our house motion pictures always seemed as magical as the airplane, the telephone, electricity, and indoor plumbing.

When I was in high school, I did not realize when we took class trips to theaters in downtown Detroit to see *West Side Story* and *The Sound of Music* that I was living through a golden age of film musicals.

What I loved about musicals as a young adult is the way they transported me away from our farm to worlds that I never imagined or thought I would never see. You could be vicariously an American in Paris, a nun in the Alps, or a visitor in the "merry old land of Oz." It was also possible through musicals to live in a world where men sang and danced and joked together instead of fighting and killing one another. Even as you watch *West Side Story,* with its gang warfare and ethnic hatred, you are aware that the fights and murders are being staged as an excuse to sing and dance. At the end of *West Side Story*, *The King and I*, and even *The Music Man*, it is uplifting to see ego, greed, jealousy, and rage defeated by a song.

The preferences you develop and favorites you have as a young adult stay with you forever. Judy Garland was the most mesmerizing performer I had ever seen. Something about her led me to all the rest of the stars of the 1940s, and I was mistakenly convinced that I was the only teenager in the rural Midwest who appreciated Judy Garland. I still like the athletic Gene Kelly a bit better than the debonair Fred Astaire. I prefer the Doris Day–type heroine who brought out the best in her man (*Young at Heart*) over the Debbie Reynolds schemer gal, who was often trying to trick a man (*Singin' in the Rain*). Then there was adorable Shirley Temple, who sang and danced in almost all of her films. She can still stop me in my tracks when I see her on the screen.

It was long after my musical preferences were set that I learned that certain singers' voices were dubbed in films—usually the women's. Both Fred Astaire and Gene Kelly had rather thin voices, but to my knowledge they were never dubbed. Audrey Hepburn's singing in *My Fair Lady* was dubbed, even though she had a perfectly nice voice. The same is true of Natalie Wood in *West Side Story* and Ava Gardner in *Show Boat*. But it was not until I watched *South Pacific* recently that I better understood why dubbing is not such a travesty. Hollywood musicals are about the movie as a whole package, not about the star's ability to sing a solo live on stage. Mitzi Gaynor had the right look and acting talent for *South Pacific*, and you would never know from her performance that the voice is not her own.

How do you measure a musical's greatness? Most often it depends on when you saw the movie. Recall the librarian's mantra: "The right movie for the right viewer at the right time." Do you leave the experience with melodies going round and round in your head? Does the music move the story along? After a dozen viewings, can the movie still make you cry or laugh? For me, *The Wizard of Oz*, yes. *The Sound of Music*, yes. *Meet Me in St. Louis*, yes. *Repo! The Genetic Opera*, maybe not so much.

The monumentally successful musicals of Richard Rodgers and Oscar Hammerstein II may seem saccharine, but they revere and simultaneously poke fun at some of America's most valued institutions, drawing attention to some of their harmful shortcomings. This explains the appeal of *State Fair*, *The Sound of Music*, *Flower Drum Song*, and *Oklahoma!*, with their affectionate ribbing of rural life, ethnicity, and even religion. Watch *Calamity*

*Jane* for another example; everyone gets ribbed—women, cowboys, Indians. A sense of the absurd helps when you watch musical comedy.

When you look back at the golden age of movie musicals, many of which were adapted from successful Broadway shows, it's surprising to note how many of the most powerful ones attempt to address the issue of racism. *Show Boat, South Pacific,* and *Porgy and Bess* are not about race directly but are still full of clues about being black in segregated, racist, white America. Watch the American musicals of the pre–civil rights era and you can observe four distinct treatments of black people: (1) complete exclusion, (2) inclusion but in stereotypical roles, (3) relegation to specialty numbers showcasing real talent that could be excised for screening in the South, and (4) imitation by white performers in blackface performing in that bizarre American musical form known as the minstrel show. However, in some films, notably those directed by Vincente Minnelli, talented black performers are presented with dignity, if not equality.

The great songwriter Irving Berlin once said, "History makes music and music makes history." In the book *The American Songbook: The Singers, the Songwriters, and the Songs,* the avid contemporary chronicler of popular music Michael Feinstein observed, "While I'd never consider it a requirement that everyone be a walking syllabus of popular standards, I feel that we are in danger of losing something essential when our past is not celebrated and appreciated by today's audiences." Film librarians, archivists, and preservationists couldn't agree more.

Somewhere around 1975, the introduction of the videocassette recorder enabled libraries to own and circulate movies just as they did books. Before then, only large libraries or archives could own copies of films, and they lent them only to institutions that owned the equipment with which to screen them. The VCR revolutionized access to films, and access has only gotten better and better with each new technology. But the more available entertainment becomes, the more urgent the need to determine which musicals to watch. Recommendations from friends are one way to learn, but recommendations from your community librarians are even better, because librarians are trained to match people with the information they need and want. So ask about musicals at your library.

Many of the films on my must-see list have been remastered and re-released on DVD, with scene selection, audio commentary, a still-photo gallery, and the original theatrical trailer to make it easier to learn about these movies in the context of their times. Some musicals originally made in black-

and-white have been colorized. Watching musicals and learning about them will help you and your family develop an understanding of the conventions that ruled Hollywood through the decades.

Film preservation is a top priority at the Library of Congress, the national library of the United States. The library's National Film Preservation Board annually selects titles to be added to the National Film Registry. The National Film Preservation Foundation is the nonprofit organization created by the U.S. Congress to help save America's film heritage. It supports activities nationwide that preserve American films and improve film access for study, education, and exhibition. Musical feature films that have already been added to the National Film Registry are noted in this book. Anyone can nominate movies for consideration by visiting http://loc.gov/film/vote.html and filling out a nomination form.

In some ways, I'm glad I had to sneak around to watch old movies when I was a child; it made the discoveries that much more thrilling. But I also wish that I'd had access to all of these films and their great creators much earlier, as we do now, through libraries, Amazon.com, the Internet Movie Database, public television, and nonprofit archives such as Facets Multimedia. I am certain that if I had been able to watch Judy Garland and Gene Kelly, Jeanette MacDonald and Nelson Eddy, and Fred Astaire and Ginger Rogers singing those famous songs on YouTube, I would have been up all night doing exactly that—and hoping nobody would try to stop me.

The result of a lifetime of loving musicals, what follows is an assessment of the best, the most interesting, and the most representative examples of their times. My choices for the very best musicals are presented in gray boxes. Once you've seen those, you may find yourself hooked. When you have seen all the must-see films on my list, you can consider yourself a graduate of the American Library Association College of Musical Knowledge!

## KEY TO SYMBOLS

🎞️ Included in the National Film Registry

☻ Animated

📷 Biography

☐ Every movie has a box for you to check when you've seen the film

★BEST of the BEST★ The very best on this must-see musicals list are set off in gray boxes.

# ALL-TALKING, ALL-SINGING, ALL-DANCING, ALL-MIXED-UP

HEN YOU WATCH THESE EARLY MUSICALS, notice how the singing and dancing are often filmed as if they were being performed on stage, with the camera being merely a substitute for a seated live audience. During this period, musicals were mostly variety shows with cockamamie plots holding the acts together. Exceptions to this format can be seen in operettas such as *Naughty Marietta*, which features the legendary singing duo Jeanette MacDonald and Nelson Eddy in realistic settings. I have to admit that if fast-forward had existed when I first watched many of the musicals of the 1930s, I would have used it to speed past some of the dialogue that fills the space between production numbers.

Filmmaking itself had just begun around the turn of the twentieth century; movies were silent and shown with live musical accompaniment in local movie theaters. When movies began to talk in the late 1920s, the musical was born, and *The Jazz Singer* is credited with starting the sound revolution. Busby Berkeley became the director and choreographer who most experimented with what the big screen could do; lavish, kaleidoscopic, precisely choreographed song-and-dance sequences characterize his direction.

In the mid-1930s, the censorious Motion Picture Production Code (also known as the Hays Code) began controlling the content of most movies in the United States. Movies made before the Hays Code are often risqué, witty, sophisticated, and laced with double entendre, with stars like Mae West bumping and grinding her way through comedy films that pushed puritanical buttons.

Although film techniques were still evolving, a couple of all-time great film musicals premiered during the 1930s—the authentically revolutionary *Show Boat* and the authentically weird *The Wizard of Oz*. I remember seeing the latter in a movie theater as a preschooler and being terrified, not by the witch or the flying monkeys, but by the tornado. Did you know that the tornado scene was done with muslin and wind machines and that Judy Garland singing "Over the Rainbow" was almost cut from the film?

## ☐ THE JAZZ SINGER (1927) ▦

Even though it is essentially a silent picture, this film gets the credit for revolutionizing movies and ushering in "talkies." Its star, Al Jolson, was already a vaudeville legend and, at age forty, really too old for the part of a rebellious Jewish youth who's forced to leave home to pursue his dream, but audiences were thrilled when he opened his mouth and songs came out. Among the best in the film are "Blue Skies," "Mammy," and "Toot, Toot Tootsie!" While this film is essential viewing when learning about musicals, it seems at best a curiosity, and Jolson singing in blackface is more ridiculous than charming today. It's ironic that the first sound musical featured a white Jew imitating African American performance style for a primarily WASP audience, setting up America's racial divide as a subtext or theme in musicals for years to come. The wildly popular Jolson quickly made four more similar films—*The Singing Fool* (1928), *Say It with Songs* (1929), and *Mammy* and *Big Boy* (1930). Other noteworthy Jolson flicks, such as *Hallelujah I'm a Bum* (1933) and *Go Into Your Dance* (1935) give more insight into his talent and the great songs he popularized. *The Jazz Singer* was remade in 1953 with Danny Thomas in the lead; it's worth seeing if you remember TV's *Make Room for Daddy* and for a rare film role by the incomparable singer Peggy Lee. It was also remade in 1980 with Neil Diamond, but that version is worth seeing only if you are a devoted Diamond fan.

The New York premiere of *The Jazz Singer*

## ☐ THE BROADWAY MELODY (1929)

Significant as the first real Hollywood musical, this Metro-Goldwyn-Mayer (MGM) production featured music by Nacio Herb Brown and Arthur Freed, including the film's biggest hit, "You Were Meant for Me." Freed stayed on at MGM and was responsible for some of the studio's most successful musicals, continuing into the 1950s.

## ☐ THE DESERT SONG (1929)

Warner Bros. studios produced this first screen operetta, largely a film version of a Sigmund Romberg stage operetta with some added outdoor scenes. Watching the film gives you a real sense of the times in which it was made, what audiences responded to, and how thrilling sound must have been in early talkies. John Boles and Carlotta King earnestly trill their way through the movie, clips of which are readily available on YouTube. The movie was redone in 1953 with Kathryn Grayson and Gordon MacRae, and their romantic duet of the title song is beautifully filmed, demonstrating how far filmmaking had come in less than a quarter of a century. Both versions reflect the public's ongoing fascination with exotic portrayals of sheiks and all things Arab.

☐ **GOLD DIGGERS OF BROADWAY** (1929)

This musical comedy was the third movie released by Warner Bros. in color, and it was a box office smash, making Winnie Lightner a star and bringing greater fame to guitarist-crooner Nick Lucas as he sang two songs that became twentieth-century standards: "Tiptoe through the Tulips" and "Painting the Clouds with Sunshine."

☐ **HALLELUJAH** (1929) ▦

This clichéd and stereotypical film nevertheless represents a sincere effort on the part of director King Vidor to draw attention to the lives of poor black people in the American South. The film showcases traditional spirituals, including "Sometimes I Feel like a Motherless Child," "Go Down Moses (Let My People Go)," "Swing Low, Sweet Chariot," "Get on Board, Little Children," and "Gimme Dat Old Time Religion," along with "Waiting at the End of the Road" and "Swanee Shuffle" by Irving Berlin, "St. Louis Blues" by W. C. Handy, and "Old Folks at Home" by Stephen Foster. It's also interesting to note that the film's star, Nina Mae McKinney, was the first black woman to be offered a contract by a major Hollywood studio, MGM.

☐ **THE HOLLYWOOD REVUE OF 1929**

The well-known song "Singin' in the Rain" was introduced not in the 1952 movie of the same name, but here, played during the opening by the MGM Symphony Orchestra, then on the ukulele and sung by Cliff Edwards and the Brox Sisters, and reprised by the major stars at the end. This enormously successful variety show featured American songs written by nineteenth-century composer Stephen Foster, "Old Folks at Home" and "Old Black Joe," reviving interest in that bizarre and racist American entertainment form known as the minstrel show. This film also features dramatic actress Joan Crawford singing and dancing "Gotta Feelin' for You" (and offering pretty clear proof for why she stuck with acting). "You Were Meant for Me" is another fine featured tune that has held up well over time, and the John Philip Sousa marches "The Stars and Stripes Forever" and "The Washington Post" are used to great effect. This film intentionally lacks a story line; rather, it served as a showcase for the MGM contract players of the time, which even included comedian Jack Benny and the immortal comedy team Laurel and Hardy.

## ☐ ON WITH THE SHOW! (1929)

This was the first all-color, all-talking musical feature, and the best thing about it is watching the brilliant Ethel Waters sing "Am I Blue?" In the second half of the number, Waters is accompanied by the Harmony Four Quartette. A victim of the haphazard early efforts of American film preservation, copies of this movie survive only in black-and-white.

## ☐ RIO RITA (1929)

Hollywood's second all-color, all-talking feature film broke all box office records and for ten years after remained the highest grossing film ever produced. In it, moviegoers first heard Bebe Daniels's singing voice on the silver screen, and it was a sensation. Teaming her with handsome John Boles proved to be good casting, because he also had a wonderful singing voice. Their duet in counterpoint at the beginning of the film (he sings the title tune while she sings "River Song") must have made audiences swoon. You really have to project yourself back in time to appreciate this one.

## ☐ SUNNY SIDE UP (1929)

Notable for its ridiculous musical number "Turn On the Heat," this film also serves as a great example of the talents and appeal of Janet Gaynor, one of the most popular and versatile actresses of her time, who retired from films in 1938 at the age of thirty-two. She sings the title tune, which became a real anthem of optimism during the Great Depression.

## ☐ THE BLUE ANGEL (1930)

This is not a musical, but it is a must-see because of the classic moment in cinema history when Marlene Dietrich sings "Falling in Love Again (Can't Help It)" and Emil Jannings's obsession with her begins reducing him from distinguished professor to cabaret clown.

## ☐ KING OF JAZZ (1930)

One of the first films to use an editing technique that made the camera keep better time with the music, this film showcases popular Paul Whiteman and his band playing songs that are largely unheard today, with the possible exception of "Mississippi Mud." Look for Bing Crosby as one of the Rhythm

Boys. It was his first screen appearance, before it was clear that he would become one of the most enduring leading men in twentieth-century movies.

☐ **A LADY'S MORALS** (1930) 📷

Metropolitan Opera soprano Grace Moore stars in this melodramatic biopic loosely based on the life of Jenny Lind. Known as "the Swedish nightingale," Lind was an enormously popular opera singer in the nineteenth century, made even more so when she toured America under the direction of the great circus man P. T. Barnum.

☐ **WHOOPEE!** (1930)

*Whoopee!* is considered a turning point in the development of film musicals, when they stopped being stage productions on film. Thanks are due to the arrival of Busby Berkeley, the most influential choreographer of all time, who directed and edited lavish production numbers in entirely new ways, including using color. This film also offers insight into the popularity of Eddie Cantor, whose appeal is not always easy to fathom today. He sings "Makin' Whoopee!" and "My Baby Just Cares for Me," songs so clever and singable that they have became American standards. Brace yourself again for the bizarre and racist convention of blackface, in which white performers blacken their faces and behave like Negro stereotypes, a practice that pervaded Hollywood musicals through their first thirty years. The film and song also established "makin' whoopee" as a permanent euphemism for "making love."

☐ **THE SMILING LIEUTENANT** (1931)

Maurice Chevalier stars in this romantic comedy directed by the great Ernst Lubitsch. One of the most memorable songs is "Jazz Up Your Lingerie," during which costar Miriam Hopkins burns her underwear in the fireplace.

☐ **THE THREEPENNY OPERA** (1931)

Not the first musical one should see when studying the history of musical films, this German curiosity nevertheless features the classic "Mack the Knife." It was also released in French as a completely separate film with a different cast. It's worth hearing in German and marveling at the fact that this classic collaboration between Kurt Weill and Bertolt Brecht was released in 1931, when Germany was already rumbling with the rise of the Nazis, who banned the film. Set in England, it's a dark story about a murderer, a real contrast to the happy-go-lucky musicals that Hollywood was producing, in complete

*Whoopee!* features lavish production numbers choreographed by Busby Berkeley.

denial of what was going on in Europe. Lotte Lenya is one of the stars, and if you listen to the popular English-language version of "Mack the Knife," you'll notice that the actress became part of the lyrics. This is definitely a film for the advanced movie scholar. In 1990 an American version (renamed *Mack the Knife*) was released, starring the often-underrated Raul Julia, Richard Harris, Julie Walters, and Roger Daltrey. It's more fun to watch than the 1931 version.

☐ **THE BIG BROADCAST** (1932)
An interesting example of the filmed radio broadcasts that were popular in the 1930s, this movie offers dozens of performers who were enormously popular in their day singing songs that became standards in the American songbook or doing the shticks for which they were famous. Among the best are Kate Smith singing "It Was So Beautiful," bandleader Cab Calloway's "Minnie the Moocher," and Bing Crosby crooning his classic "When the Blue of the Night (Meets the Gold of the Day)."

☐ **BLONDE VENUS** (1932)
This iconic melodrama is the kind of film that makes Marlene Dietrich and Cary Grant Hollywood icons. Dietrich's performance as a cabaret singer in a blond afro singing "Hot Voodoo" is over the top.

☐ **LOVE ME TONIGHT** (1932)
Teaming Jeanette MacDonald and Maurice Chevalier, with Rouben Mamoulian directing, this musical is an early example of the effective integration of dialogue, song, and scoring. The music, by the inspired team of Richard Rodgers and Lorenz Hart, is a preview of greater things to come when Rodgers would team with Oscar Hammerstein II. MacDonald's rendition of "Lover" is a magic moment, and Chevalier sings the great "Isn't It Romantic?" and his signature song "Mimi." Chevalier had enormous influence on and an enduring career in musicals over four decades.

☐ **ONE HOUR WITH YOU** (1932)
Maurice Chevalier and Jeanette MacDonald are once again paired in this racy romantic comedy that plays fast and loose with infidelity. Listen for their duet "What a Little Thing like a Wedding Ring Can Do."

☐ **DUCK SOUP** (1933) ▦
Without highbrow Margaret Dumont as the unwitting butt of their jokes, the Marx Brothers—Groucho, Harpo, Chico, and Zeppo—wouldn't have been half as entertaining. As the imperious dowager, she is a striking contrast to their nonsense, totally oblivious to Groucho's puns and sarcasm. "This is a gala day for you," says Dumont. "Well a gal a day is enough for me. I don't think I could handle any more," Groucho snaps. Apropos of nothing, people break into song, and the make-believe country of Freedonia erupts in chaos at the hands of President Rufus T. Firefly, played by Groucho. "Why, a four-year-old child could understand this report," he says. "Run out and find me a four-year-old child; I can't make head or tail of it." This is not a musical in any true sense of the word, but there are plenty of familiar tunes and obscure musical references to satisfy your curiosity about how well these zany comedians hold up.

☐ **FLYING DOWN TO RIO** (1933)
This energetic film features some musical daredevil stunts by beautiful women on an airplane. It also features the first pairing of dance sensations Fred Astaire and Ginger Rogers, who do not get top billing in the film—that honor goes to the beautiful Dolores del Rio. There's never been a better example of the styles and conventions of the 1930s or American audiences' fascination with Latin America. Be sure to catch African American singer and

actress Etta Moten as one of the Brazilian entertainers singing "The Carioca," while Fred and Ginger dance.

### ☐ FOOTLIGHT PARADE (1933) ▦

Billed as "the greatest musical extravaganza of them all," *Footlight Parade* puts James Cagney in the lead role, singing and dancing along with the superb Joan Blondell and Ruby Keeler, straight out of *42nd Street*. The songs and dances are unforgettable, especially as they are supposedly being performed on a stage. "By a Waterfall" boasts three hundred girls in a Busby Berkeley number that defies logic, as there is no way, with all those girls and all that water, it could have been performed on stage. But who cares? Cagney and Keeler are at their best in "Shanghai Lil," and Blondell is sharp and saucy in one of her best screen roles. Ever-reliable Dick Powell also delivers the goods in his cocky style, singing "Honeymoon Hotel" with Keeler in a clever and naughty vignette.

### ☐ 42ND STREET (1933) ▦

This is the one that started it all, from the catchy title song to Warner Baxter's advice to newbie Ruby Keeler as she steps in for the star of a show who has broken her ankle: "You're going out a youngster, but you've got to come back

Warner Baxter, Ruby Keeler, Bebe Daniels, and Dick Powell star in *42nd Street*.

a star!" Bebe Daniels sings the classic "You're Getting to Be a Habit with Me," and nearly twenty minutes of the movie are devoted to three Busby Berkeley production numbers: "Shuffle Off to Buffalo," "Young and Healthy," and the title song. The lavish sets paid off, with high profits and a lasting legacy that has brought talented hopefuls to New York ever since (even though it was filmed entirely in California).

## ☐ GOLD DIGGERS OF 1933 ▦

This film contains four song-and-dance sequences designed, staged, and choreographed by Busby Berkeley: "We're in the Money" sung by Ginger Rogers, accompanied by scantily clad showgirls dancing with giant coins (note that Rogers sings one verse in pig Latin, which was all the rage with young people at the time); "Pettin' in the Park," with Ruby Keeler and Dick Powell, which includes a tap dance by Keeler and a surreal section featuring a dwarf actor as a baby who escapes from his stroller; "Shadow Waltz," sung by Powell and Keeler and featuring a dance by Keeler, Rogers, and many female violinists with neon-tubed violins that glow in the dark; and "Remember My Forgotten Man," recited by Joan Blondell and sung by Etta Moten (with some question remaining over what parts of whose voice were dubbed by the legendary Marian Anderson). Sets influenced by German Expressionism evoke Depression-era poverty. It is said that Berkeley was inspired by the May 1932 war veterans' march on Washington, D.C. Trite it may be, but this is the best segment in the film.

## ☐ SHE DONE HIM WRONG (1933) ▦

Although this really cannot be classified as a musical, it is a classic example of Mae West at her suggestive best and of what movie audiences considered naughty in 1933. West costars with the extraordinary Cary Grant and sings three noteworthy songs: "I Wonder Where My Easy Rider's Gone," "A Guy What Takes His Time," and "Frankie and Johnnie."

## ☐ BELLE OF THE NINETIES (1934)

Mae West's mere dozen motion pictures were mostly comedies, but they generally included her shimmying languorously though a song or two. Musically, this is probably the best Mae West film, notable for the inclusion of the Duke Ellington Orchestra. It was the first time a white singer shared the screen democratically with black musicians, and it's said that West fought hard to make it happen. With Ellington's orchestra backing her up, she sings "Memphis Blues," "Troubled Waters," and the unforgettable "My Old Flame." She was ahead of her time in almost every way, a one-woman liberation movement who wrote her own material, including plays dealing with everything from interracial love to homosexuality. The Hays Code almost did her in, but no survey of musicals would be complete without the inclusion of Mae West.

☐ **THE CAT AND THE FIDDLE** (1934)
Although seldom watched today, this romantic romp about two composers is notable for at least three reasons: First, the magnificent voice of Jeanette MacDonald, before she became famous for duets with frequent costar Nelson Eddy; second, the appearance of a singing Ramon Novarro, a popular Latin-lover type in silent films; and third, the shift at the end of the film into an early use of then-innovative Technicolor.

☐ **DAMES** (1934)
In one of his best musicals, Dick Powell sings "I Only Have Eyes for You" with Ruby Keeler, in another Busby Berkeley spectacle. The great Joan Blondell costars, but it is the kaleidoscopic production numbers that make this worth seeing, especially the title tune with all the girls at their toilette.

☐ **THE GAY DIVORCEE** (1934)
This Fred Astaire–Ginger Rogers pairing peaks with their dance to Cole Porter's beautiful "Night and Day." There has never been a dance number more delightful or a tune catchier than "The Continental" played out on those beautiful art deco sets.

☐ **HOLLYWOOD PARTY** (1934)
The hilarious Jimmy Durante, known for making fun of his own large schnozzola, sings his signature song in this film, "Inka Dinka Doo." Along the way you'll hear some great songs by Richard Rodgers and Lorenz Hart (from before Rodgers teamed with Oscar Hammerstein II to create some of America's greatest musicals), including the title song performed by Frances Williams, "Reincarnation" performed by Durante, and "Hello" performed by Durante and Jack Pearl.

## ☐ KID MILLIONS (1934)

There is no better example of Hollywood nonsense than this comedy with the bewilderingly popular Eddie Cantor. The jokes are so outrageous and politically incorrect that the film is mesmerizing, as you look back at the times. The Goldwyn Girls and the brilliant dancing Nicholas Brothers stand out in this film, and the classic song "Mandy" also features Ethel Merman, Ann Sothern, George Murphy, and Cantor inexplicably wearing blackface minstrel makeup.

## ☐ THE MERRY WIDOW (1934)

This classic operetta contains what is probably the best musical sequence in any film by director Ernst Lubitsch, namely the scene in Maxim's. It's an Americanized glorification of Paris that includes the cancan and Mr. France himself, Maurice Chevalier. The women in the film all go gaga for Chevalier, and though his charms may escape you, he performs up a storm in this comic romance and somehow manages to convince all the women in the film, and the audience, that he loves them all. "The Merry Widow Waltz" is a standout, and the black-and-white costumes and sets are a visual feast. Beauti-

Jeanette MacDonald and Maurice Chevalier in *The Merry Widow*

ful Jeanette MacDonald costars and does most of the singing in the film. *The Merry Widow* was remade in 1952, starring Fernando Lamas and Lana Turner (dubbed), with Broadway legend Gwen Verdon dancing the cancan.

### ☐ WE'RE NOT DRESSING (1934)

This screwball comedy starring Bing Crosby, Carole Lombard (queen of screwballs), and Ethel Merman is an escapist romp on a deserted island that features plenty of music, not much of which is remembered today. Where does the orchestration come from, anyway? All the more reason to see this movie. In addition, "Love Thy Neighbor" ought to be remembered—and practiced—more today. All that's required to enjoy it is a sense of fun and the suspension of disbelief. Crosby's career in films extended for more than forty years, and he is one of the all-time top box office attractions.

### ☐ WONDER BAR (1934)

"Why can't this go on forever?" asks gorgeous Dolores del Rio, later a casualty of Hollywood conservatism, in this pre–Production Code spectacular from Busby Berkeley that features two men dancing off together as Al Jolson quips, "Boys will be boys, wooo!" Ever-charming Dick Powell sings the memorable title song.

### ☐ GOLD DIGGERS OF 1935

Busby Berkeley's exuberant song and dance "Lullaby of Broadway" makes this film memorable. Dick Powell was the darling of audiences in the 1930s, with his cocky optimism. The piano sequence is visually stunning; with its art deco sets, it is also an illustration of urban isolationism and conveys the mood of the Great Depression. Watch as the song moves dreamily along, and then leaves you with a disturbing conclusion. If you liked *Titanic* (1997), watch for a young Gloria Stuart in this film as the rich girl who sings "I'm Going Shopping with You" with Powell.

### ☐ THE LITTLE COLONEL (1935)

Though really a comedy-drama that focuses on the reconciliation of an estranged father and daughter in the years following the American Civil War, the film pairs Shirley Temple with Bill "Bojangles" Robinson in the first of four cinematic pairings between Robinson and the most successful child star of all time. Most of Temple's films contain a song and dance or two, and this one features the duo's famous staircase dance.

☐ **NAUGHTY MARIETTA** (1935) 🎞️
For some insight into how people endured the Great Depression, consider the glorious voices of Jeanette MacDonald and Nelson Eddy, the setting of New Orleans in 1780, and the gaiety of a Victor Herbert operetta—the perfect escape. Audiences flocked to movie palaces all over America for this, the first of eight films to pair MacDonald and Eddy in an unabashedly romantic escapade. The classic "Ah, Sweet Mystery of Life" is the best of the songs, the "Italian Street Song" is great fun, and you can't help loving Eddy singing "Tramp! Tramp! Tramp!" (which refers to marching and has nothing to do with the ladies who have been taken captive by pirates). Favorite Nelson Eddy line: "Here's to men who love a fight!"

☐ **A NIGHT AT THE OPERA** (1935) 🎞️
The Marx Brothers' comedy shtick stems mostly from mocking pretentiousness, formality, and manners. This was one of their biggest successes. After all, what would the average American want to see ridiculed more than opera? Nevertheless, most of the Marx Brothers' films had musical numbers in them, and this one has Allan Jones singing the wonderful "Alone." Also, numbers performed by Chico Marx on the piano and Harpo Marx on the harp reveal their true feelings about serious music.

☐ **ROBERTA** (1935)
Irene Dunne gets top billing over Fred Astaire and Ginger Rogers in this adaptation of a Broadway theater musical. Rogers is at her funniest, doing several dance numbers in which she outdoes Astaire. The film features Jerome Kern's timeless song "Smoke Gets in Your Eyes," as well as his "I Won't Dance" and "Lovely to Look At." *Roberta* is the third Astaire-Rogers film, and the only one to be remade with other actors. MGM did so in 1952, titling the new Technicolor version *Lovely to Look At*. With an eye to a remake, MGM had bought *Roberta* in 1945, keeping this version off the market until the 1970s.

☐ **TOP HAT** (1935) 🎞️
Ginger Rogers and Fred Astaire's fourth movie together was a huge box office success. The second biggest moneymaker of the year, it broke records at Radio City Music Hall and even earned an Academy Award nomination in the best picture category. Music and lyrics, by one of America's greatest songwriters, Irving Berlin, include such classics as "Cheek to Cheek" and "Alexander's Ragtime Band."

Ginger Rogers and Fred Astaire in *Top Hat*

### ☐ **BORN TO DANCE** (1936)

Cole Porter's marvelous songs run through this movie, with the remarkable Eleanor Powell bringing a new kind of athletic, syncopated dancing to the screen, rendering earlier dance musicals clunky in comparison. In fact, there has never been a better dancer on screen than Powell. And be sure to listen for one of the greatest Porter songs ever, "I've Got You under My Skin." You may also recognize a young singer-dancer, Buddy Ebsen, who later achieved television fame as Jed Clampett in *The Beverly Hillbillies*.

### ☐ **FOLLOW THE FLEET** (1936)

Don't miss this performance of the greatest dance partners in screen history. Fred Astaire and Ginger Rogers add luster to a typically screwball plot with a slew of Irving Berlin classics, including "Let's Face the Music and Dance." If you like this movie, try *The Fleet's In* (1942), starring Dorothy Lamour and William Holden and introducing the unforgettable "I Remember You."

☐ **THE GREAT ZIEGFELD** (1936) 🔲
In a black-and-white re-creation of the 1893 Chicago World's Fair, the great showman Florenz Ziegfeld (portrayed by William Powell) begins his show business career by cashing in on the sex appeal of German bodybuilder Eugen Sandow. This successful biopic shows how the impresario made and lost many fortunes, each time investing in a newer, more spectacular show, leading to the Ziegfeld Follies, which were re-created for the movie. The film balances Ziegfeld's charm with his unbridled drive and shows how difficult it was to be married to a man who made it his work to "glorify the American girl." One of the best reasons to watch this film is to see the real glory that was Fanny Brice, as she plays herself and performs "Yiddle on Your Fiddle," "Queen of the Jungle," and the classic "My Man." These rare film cameos give you some insight into her phenomenal popularity and how she compares to Barbra Streisand's portrayal of her in the biopic musical *Funny Girl*. There's plenty of music in this film, an Oscar-winning performance by Luise Rainer, and another top-notch performance by the fabulous Myrna Loy. You'll also spot Ray Bolger (doing the splits like you've never seen) and Frank Morgan in this film, soon to appear in *The Wizard of Oz*. In addition, Dennis Morgan sings "A Pretty Girl Is like a Melody." This is one of the most interesting and watchable biopics ever.

☐ **POOR LITTLE RICH GIRL** (1936)
Shirley Temple is at her most endearing in this film under the care of the great Alice Faye and Jack Haley. More musical than most of her films, this one features the songs "Oh, My Goodness!" (Shirley's trademark line), "You've Gotta Eat Your Spinach, Baby," and "But Definitely."

☐ **ROSE-MARIE** (1936)
This has to be one of the best of the eight film pairings of Jeanette MacDonald and Nelson Eddy. "Indian Love Call" has been parodied so many times that it helps to hear the original, and you will find it calling you-oo-oo-oo-oo-oo-oo back to this film for its production values, its earnest romanticism, and the sight of Eddy in his Canadian Mounties uniform. The opera within the operetta gives MacDonald and Allan Jones an opportunity to sing parts of Charles Gounod's *Romeo et Juliette*. Watch for early screen appearances of David Niven and James Stewart. It's also interesting to note that the opulence of the sets was exactly what people wanted to see on screen during the Great Depression.

★BEST *of the* BEST★

## ☐ SHOW BOAT (1936) 🎞

*Show Boat* began in 1927 as a revolutionary stage musical, with music by Jerome Kern and book and lyrics by Oscar Hammerstein II. Based on Edna Ferber's best-selling novel of the same name, the musical follows the lives of the performers, stagehands, and dockworkers on the *Cotton Blossom*, a showboat on the Mississippi River, beginning in the late nineteenth century. With themes including racial prejudice and

Paul Robeson, Irene Dunne, Hattie McDaniel, and Helen Morgan

enduring love, the musical contributed such classic songs as "Ol' Man River," "Make Believe," and "Can't Help Lovin' Dat Man" to the American songbook. The arrival of *Show Boat* was a historic moment in the history of American theater. The show was a radical departure in musical storytelling and rose above the operettas and light musicals that were in vogue at the time, and it was an equally radical concept when applied to film. Popular Irene Dunne stars, playing Magnolia, with Helen Morgan as Julie and Paul Robeson as Joe, who sings "Ol' Man River."

## ☐ SAN FRANCISCO (1936)

Set in San Francisco just before the catastrophic earthquake of 1906 that destroyed the city, the film is not really a musical; rather, it's a drama constructed to showcase the special effects used to re-create the great quake, along with the acting and singing talents of silken-voiced Jeanette MacDonald. Her rendering of the title song while standing in the ruins of the city is a classic movie moment. Clark Gable plays the owner of a bawdy music hall, which is the excuse to set MacDonald singing. Note that MacDonald claims her virtuous credentials by explaining to Gable that she worked at the public library before she got a job singing.

## ☐ SWING TIME (1936) 🎞

Everything that was perfect about the film pairing of Fred Astaire and Ginger Rogers is on display in this black-and-white delight sprinkled with clever memorable tunes, including "Pick Yourself Up," "A Fine Romance," and the

Oscar-winning "The Way You Look Tonight." The score is by the legendary Jerome Kern and Dorothy Fields, and the dancing is incomparable in the history of cinema. Rogers's dancing in her gowns is poetry in motion. She brings to mind the famous comment about the disproportionate praise lavished on Astaire for his dancing, "Sure he was great, but don't forget that Ginger Rogers did everything he did, backwards . . . and in high heels!"

☐ **THREE SMART GIRLS** (1936)
Deanna Durbin was enormously popular for about a decade, and this was her first feature-length film. Watching it will give you some insight into Durbin's international fame. Her popularity was so widespread that diarist Anne Frank pasted her picture to her bedroom wall in the Achterhuis, where the Frank family hid during World War II. The picture can still be seen there today. Durbin is best remembered for her singing voice, variously described as being light and artless but full, sweet, and unaffected. With the skill and range of a lyric soprano, she performed everything from popular standards to operatic arias in twenty-one feature films. Try this one first.

☐ **A DAMSEL IN DISTRESS** (1937)
A silly plot by P. G. Wodehouse and a set of songs by George and Ira Gershwin form the core of this Fred Astaire vehicle, set in England. He really must have been the busiest actor in Hollywood at the time. "Nice Work If You Can Get It" and "A Foggy Day in London Town" became American standards after they were introduced in this film, which shows Astaire dancing in the streets long before Martha and the Vandellas. George Burns and Gracie Allen provide plenty of comic relief, especially singing and dancing on a rotating platform to "Keep a Stiff Upper Lip," the lyrics of which are reminiscent of Wodehouse, who actually participated in the translation of his prose to film. My favorite moment in the entire movie, however, is when Astaire sings and swings "Nice Work" with three fabulous dames.

☐ **MAYTIME** (1937)
The ghostly flower-strewn finale has been called one of motion picture history's most touching scenes, and this film may be Jeanette MacDonald and Nelson Eddy's finest two hours and thirteen minutes, enhanced by the appearance of the legendary John Barrymore (Drew's grandfather) as MacDonald's possessive voice teacher. Sigmund Romberg's beautiful theme song

"Will You Remember?" (sometimes known as "The Sweetheart Song") sticks with you long after the film ends, and the Russian opera sequence adapted from Tchaikovsky's Fifth Symphony is perhaps the best of the many superbly presented opera excerpts.

## ☐ ON THE AVENUE (1937)
Among the top reasons to see this film is to witness Dick Powell and Alice Faye singing Irving Berlin's classic "I've Got My Love to Keep Me Warm."

## ☐ SHALL WE DANCE (1937)
Ginger Rogers and Fred Astaire marked the beginning of stronger plotlines in this, the seventh of their ten films together. While some of the dance numbers may not be up to the standard the duo had set with their previous films, it's great fun watching Rogers sing the clever "They All Laughed," and the dance with Astaire that follows is adorable. Their duet "Let's Call the Whole Thing Off" is a classic, and then they dance on roller skates! Then there's "They Can't Take That Away from Me." It doesn't get any better. This is my favorite Fred and Ginger movie, all thanks to songwriters George and Ira Gershwin.

## ☐ SNOW WHITE AND THE SEVEN DWARFS (1937) ▦ 🎬
Walt Disney set the standard forever with this classic animated musical—his first—adapted from Grimm's fairy tales and filmed in Technicolor. The film introduced "Heigh-Ho," "With a Smile and a Song," "Whistle While You Work," and "Some Day My Prince Will Come" into the American musical repertoire.

## ☐ ALEXANDER'S RAGTIME BAND (1938)
With music by the incomparable Irving Berlin, this pre–World War II ditty in black-and-white tells the story of a classical musician, played by handsome and sensitive Tyrone Power, who rejects the good life for ragtime. Highlights include a great turkey trot dance sequence to "Everybody's Doin' It Now," "When the Midnight Choo Choo Leaves for Alabam'," "Oh! How I Hate to Get Up in the Morning," "Remember," Ethel Merman singing "Say It with Music," "A Pretty Girl Is like a Melody," "Blue Skies," "Heat Wave," and Don Ameche singing "Easter Parade." A great story line makes this movie even more watchable. On the eve of World War II it is—not accidentally—full of American optimism and packed with more great songs than any movie has a right to be.

Eleanor Powell and George Murphy in *Broadway Melody of 1938*

## ☐ THE BIG BROADCAST OF 1938

The star of this film is an obnoxious W. C. Fields, who neither sings nor dances (thank goodness) and whose comic appeal is often hard to fathom. A sea cruise is the excuse for Bob Hope to emcee the big broadcast as it transmits from a ship. Along the way, you'll see Shep Fields and His Rippling Rhythm Orchestra display an early use of animation in a charming sequence that has a drop of water jumping around the musicians. You get treated to some painful slapstick and sing-yelling by Martha Raye, as well as two numbers by Mexican singer Tito Guizar, whose classical voice training is apparent. You can distract (or depress) yourself picking out all the racist moments in the film, such as Fields referring to a baby seal as a pickaninny. Also featured is the song that became Bob Hope's theme song, "Thanks for the Memory," a duet with Shirley Ross. Ross's rendering of "The Waltz Lives On" is the bloated production number that concludes the film, which even features a brief African scene showing women with platter lips. While some of the humor in this movie doesn't age well, it is a showcase of the styles and conventions of its time and a preview of things to come from many of its stars.

## ☐ BROADWAY MELODY OF 1938

Eleanor Powell dances in a tuxedo to "Broadway Rhythm," Judy Garland sings "You Made Me Love You—I Didn't Want to Do It" to a photograph of Clark Gable, and Sophie Tucker sings her signature song, "Some of These Days." Then Tucker joins Garland for "Everybody Sing," and we hear that "Happy Days Are Here Again." This is another history lesson in the famous tunes of the times and the unforgettable performers who gave them to us in song and dance.

## ☐ CAREFREE (1938)

Fred Astaire and Ginger Rogers turn in another set of remarkable performances in this romantic romp replete with great Irving Berlin songs, with the unforgettable "Change Partners" being the topper.

## ☐ COLLEGE SWING (1938)

Really a variety show, written to showcase the team of George Burns and Gracie Allen, as well as Bob Hope and Edward Everett Horton and other comics of the period, this is also a great glimpse into the music of the time, with some fascinating demonstrations of swing dancing and a production number built around the silly and wonderful song "What a Rumba Does to Romance," which includes Martha Raye doing a send-up of the popular dance of the day as well as a marvelous display of timing and the dress styles of the 1930s.

☐ **GOLD DIGGERS IN PARIS** (1938)
Another Busby Berkeley spectacle, this one boasts the benign Rudy Vallee as a club owner caught up in a screwball misunderstanding that results in his chorus girls being sent to Paris (through the magic of cinema, since the cast never left the lot). The most curious aspect of the film is the disproportionate amount of screen time given to the goofy Schnicklefritz Band.

☐ **THE GREAT WALTZ** (1938) 🔲
One of the best of the many films that celebrate classical music, this biopic of Johann Strauss manages to capture the impact the music had on the people who first heard it. The film is filled with beautiful orchestration, and the incredible Luise Rainer and Miliza Korjus give performances that are too little esteemed today. Strauss is played by Fernand Gravet, an underappreciated actor who returned to France just before the Nazi occupation and eventually became a war hero.

☐ **HOLLYWOOD HOTEL** (1938)
Directed by Busby Berkeley, the movie is about a saxophonist in Benny Goodman's band who wins a talent contest and gets a ten-week contract with a film studio. Lots of misunderstandings lead to the opportunity for Dick Powell and Rosemary Lane to put on a great show. The film is best remembered for the featured song "Hooray for Hollywood" by Johnny Mercer and Richard A. Whiting, sung by Johnnie Davis and Frances Langford and accompanied by Benny Goodman and His Orchestra. Ironically, the satirical song became a standard part of Tinseltown glamour and is still hauled out regularly for award shows and celebrations, even though Mercer's lyrics contain numerous references to the phoniness of the movie industry and film stardom. This is one of the best Warner Bros. musicals of the 1930s.

☐ **MOONLIGHT SONATA** (1938) 🔲
Brilliant and internationally famous, the Polish pianist Ignacy Jan Paderewski plays himself in this biographical story of plane crash survivors who become the guests of a Swedish baroness. Interwoven throughout this gentle

tale are piano solos performed superbly by the elderly pianist in eerie black-and-white, four years before his death and two years before the Nazi invasion of his beloved homeland.

☐ **SWEETHEARTS** (1938)
Schmaltzy as Jeanette MacDonald and Nelson Eddy's many musical confections seem today, some of the great talents of the age contributed to their creation. This one, for example, was co-scripted by that great American wit Dorothy Parker. Of all the MacDonald-Eddy films, this is one of the most delightful. Watch Ray Bolger (soon to portray the scarecrow in *The Wizard of Oz*) tap his way through a Dutch-themed number. Victor Herbert's operetta *Sweethearts* is the basis for this film, in which there's more than a little anti-Hollywood sentiment, despite its lavish veneer. And MacDonald's fashion spree as she "goes Hollywood" is a lot of fun to watch.

☐ **BABES IN ARMS** (1939)
Busby Berkeley's black-and-white tribute to vaudeville features Mickey Rooney and Judy Garland (shifting to a young adult role following *The Wizard of Oz*) as young show business wannabes. With music by Richard Rodgers and Lorenz Hart, the movie features "Good Morning" (later featured in the great musical *Singin' in the Rain*) and "Where or When." The film also includes a minstrel show—that bizarre American institution that's unbearable to watch once you understand how it perpetuated racism. Rooney is often obnoxious rather than endearing as he mobilizes a small town's youngsters to put on the show, which is mercifully cut short by a thunderstorm. This movie does not stand the test of time very well—in fact, it's more a victim of its times—but Garland's rendition of "I Cried for You" gives a glimpse of things to come from this great singer. It's also illuminating to watch "God's Country," a patriotic production number, knowing that World War II is just around the corner.

☐ **ON YOUR TOES** (1939)
The main reason to see this movie is the performance of Richard Rodgers's mini-ballet, *Slaughter on Tenth Avenue*. The melody will haunt you for days, and George Balanchine choreographed the main piece for the film's star, ballerina Vera Zorina. Her costar, Eddie Albert (remember TV's *Green Acres*?), was supplied with a dancing double.

## ☐ SECOND FIDDLE (1939)

She couldn't sing, she didn't dance much, and her acting was, well, evident. Nevertheless, Sonja Henie, "Queen of the Ice," became one of the biggest box office attractions of her time as a result of the twelve movies she made between 1936 and 1948. You owe it to yourself to see at least one of these films, none of which are really musicals but which often include a lot of great music. Arguably the best of her figure skating extravaganzas is *Second Fiddle*, the story of a Minnesota schoolteacher whose talent takes her to Hollywood. Sound familiar? Henie hailed from Norway and was discovered after winning three Olympic gold medals in figure skating. The Irving Berlin score and the performances of Tyrone Power, Rudy Vallee, Mary Healy, and Edna May Oliver serve as more good reasons to watch this film. And they were right about Henie; you can't keep your eyes off her. If you like what you see, give *One in a Million* (1937) a try, a film in which Borrah Minevitch and His Harmonica Rascals provide the laughs.

## ☐ THE STORY OF VERNON AND IRENE CASTLE (1939) ▣

This was the last film Ginger Rogers and Fred Astaire would make together for RKO, their home studio during the 1930s. Unlike their other musicals, this one is a biopic in which the two play out the lives of a real ballroom dance team of the nineteen-teens, Vernon and Irene Castle. It would be ten years before Rogers and Astaire would again be paired in their tenth and final musical, MGM's *The Barkleys of Broadway*.

## ☐ **THE WIZARD OF OZ** (1939) 🎞

Generation after generation, this downright bizarre little movie continues to fascinate viewers with its imaginative and surrealistic sets and score. It has

created a cottage industry around a little girl from Kansas who ends up over the rainbow, only to find that life in a dream is as often a nightmare. What is so durable about the film is the way the elements all work together to tell a story that is enthralling no matter how many times you see it. *The Wizard of Oz* is the quintessential musical. Seeing it at just the right age somehow seems to make it watchable repeatedly at any age. The music is fully integrated into the story line. Everybody sings—except,

Judy Garland, Ray Bolger, Bert Lahr, and Jack Haley

of course, the Wicked Witch of the West and her flying monkeys. (Evil beings don't sing.) In addition to "Over the Rainbow," consider how memorable are "We're Off to See the Wizard" and "If I Only Had a Brain." Much has been written about this film, and it even spawned a reworked version, *The Wiz*, starring Diana Ross, and a Broadway play, *Wicked*, but there is simply no equaling the original. And look at the casting: Judy Garland seems too old to play Dorothy—until you think that a girl going through puberty on a prairie farm, with no parents and no playmates except for "three shiftless farmhands," might be the perfect candidate for Oz. Margaret Hamilton as the Wicked Witch has defined witchiness forever, and Billie Burke's irritatingly sweet voice convinces you that she really is a witch when she tells Dorothy that she knew all along how to send her home. Ray Bolger's dance sequences as the Scarecrow are phenomenal. Jack Haley as the Tin Man is suitably sappy, and Bert Lahr couldn't have pulled off the Cowardly Lion any better than he did. (And those costumes must have been miserable to work in.) Finally, the venerable actor Frank Morgan is perfect in his blustery role as the Wizard in his various guises. By the way, if you wonder what the witch's minions are singing in the "Winkie Chant" as they march around with their spears, it's nothing more than "O-Ee-Yah! Eoh-Ah!"

# THE GREATEST GENERATION

## Patriotism, Family, and American Values

**1940s**

**T**HE MUSICALS OF THE 1940S ARE GENERALLY PATRIOTIC, wholesome, and filled with soldiers and sailors chasing pretty girls. World War II turned movie stars into morale boosters, some of whom entertained the troops in the field when they could and on film when they couldn't. Many films of this period were also designed to reassure the families left behind that "the boys" were fighting a just war that they indisputably were going to win. In those days, going to the movie theater was the equivalent of sitting down in front of the television. Audiences wanted variety, comic relief, novelty acts, and a hearty dose of sentimentality. Swing music became the soundtrack to the war, and big band leaders like Tommy Dorsey and Glenn Miller were heroes in their own right.

Outstanding in its ability to deliver patriotism and entertainment is *Yankee Doodle Dandy*, in which the multitalented James Cagney portrays songwriter George M. Cohan. As you watch the original film, it may take you a moment to realize that it is in black-and-white, a decision that has perplexed many critics, since the film is so perfect in every other way. Color was certainly available to filmmakers, as evidenced by the success of another enduring film from this period, *Meet Me in St. Louis*, starring Judy Garland and directed by the great Vincente Minnelli. Watch her sing "The Trolley Song," and compare it to "Put On Your Sunday Clothes" in *Hello, Dolly!* nearly twenty-five years later.

Two other Judy Garland films, *The Harvey Girls* and *The Pirate*, also get my vote for the best of the 1940s. Deceptively silly, both of these movies get funnier and campier with each viewing. The music in *The Harvey Girls* is especially noteworthy, and "On the Atchison, Topeka and the Santa Fe" is echoed in *Hello, Dolly!* more than thirty years later, while Gene Kelly's fantasy dance as the pirate is arguably the most breathtaking performance of his career.

## ☐ BITTER SWEET (1940)

This movie is notable for pairing the popular duet of Nelson Eddy and Jeanette MacDonald with the original play, music, and lyrics of Noël Coward, England's most renowned Renaissance man of the theater. Coward's contempt for unromantic prigs is quite apparent in his portrayal of a Victorian lass and her dashing music teacher. This is my nomination for the best of the Eddy-MacDonald films, especially for the beautiful song "I'll See You Again."

## ☐ BROADWAY MELODY OF 1940

Eleanor Powell stars opposite Fred Astaire, with an acclaimed musical score by Cole Porter. They dance to "Begin the Beguine" in what is considered by many to be one of the greatest tap sequences in film history. According to accounts of the making of this film, Astaire was somewhat intimidated by Powell, who may be the only female dancer ever capable of outdancing him. In his autobiography, *Steps in Time*, Astaire remarked, "She 'put 'em down like a man,' no ricky-ticky-sissy stuff with Ellie. She really knocked out a tap dance in a class by herself."

## ☐ DANCE, GIRL, DANCE (1940) 🎞

This is not a great musical, but you must see it for the performances of Lucille Ball (playing a character named Bubbles) and Maureen O'Hara (portraying a good girl named Judy). Ball singing and dancing the "Beer Barrel Polka" and "Jitterbug Bite" with the Bailey Brothers Burlesque Theater is worth her weight in gold. Plus, the film is directed by Dorothy Arzner, Hollywood's one female director of note between the silent era and Ida Lupino's directorial debut in 1949.

Carmen Miranda featured in *Down Argentine Way* and many more movie musicals of the 1940s.

☐ **DOWN ARGENTINE WAY** (1940)

Betty Grable and Don Ameche star in this farce, with the spectacular Carmen Miranda providing the best moments of the film. Wearing her characteristic tutti-frutti hat, Miranda starts things off with "South American Way," then "Mamãe Eu Quero" and "Bambu, Bambu." Contrary to some opinions about the Brazilian bombshell stereotype, Miranda is never the victim of the joke because she is always in on it. The joke is on the rest of the cast, since hers are the performances that endure; she can still make you laugh more than half a century after her death in 1955. And don't miss the fabulous Nicholas Brothers dancing and singing the title song in Spanish.

☐ **FANTASIA** (1940) ▦ ⚙

Mickey Mouse conducting "The Sorcerer's Apprentice" (actually Leopold Stowkowski conducting the Philadelphia Orchestra) is an unforgettable Disney moment. No one who sees it ever has quite the same attitude toward classical music. The compositions of Bach, Tchaikovsky, Stravinsky, Beethoven, and other composers seem to have been written for this film, and children will enjoy the way the animation and the music seem to be one creation. After you've seen the original, be sure to watch *Fantasia 2000* for additional fun family viewing.

☐ **LILLIAN RUSSELL** (1940) 🎦

Alice Faye is a sheer delight in this biography of singer Lillian Russell, from the protagonist's discovery in 1890 by bandleader Tony Pastor until her marriage and retirement in 1912. In between biographical moments, Faye sings the American classics that Russell made famous, including "The Band Played On" and "After the Ball."

☐ **PINOCCHIO** (1940) 🎞️ 💀

This classic animated version of the Italian fairy tale features the never-to-be-forgotten "When You Wish Upon a Star," sung by that beloved Disney character Jiminy Cricket. Some consider this story of a little wooden boy who comes to life to be Disney's finest achievement in animation. Like all good fairy tales, it has some really scary stuff in it, too.

☐ **RHYTHM ON THE RIVER** (1940)

After you've seen this, you can't say that Bing Crosby didn't do his best, in this film and in *Birth of the Blues* (1941), to give credit where credit is due for the origins of truly American music. Here he is teamed with Mary Martin, who starred in *South Pacific* when it played on Broadway. Crosby did a lot to popularize a smooth form of jazz that has helped it endure to this day and to claim its proper place in the canon. His version of the title song is a classic.

☐ **SWANEE RIVER** (1940) 🎦

The great Don Ameche stars in this fictionalized life of Stephen Foster, a songwriter from Pittsburgh who falls in love with the South and comes up with American classics like "Oh, Susanna," "Jeanie with the Light Brown Hair," "My Old Kentucky Home," "Old Black Joe," "Old Folks at Home," and "Beautiful Dreamer." Everybody should know these songs, like 'em or not.

☐ **TIN PAN ALLEY** (1940)

Alice Faye and Betty Grable team up in this costume musical as a pair of singing sisters. You have to hear the classic tune "K-K-K-Katy," sung by Jack Oakie, who uses different lyrics throughout the movie, then sung and danced at the end by the sisters on stage and by marching World War I doughboys in offstage film clips.

## ☐ TOO MANY GIRLS (1940)

There are two reasons you should haul this one out of oblivion and have a look: first, to see the legendary Lucille Ball and her future husband, Desi Arnaz, working together before television's *I Love Lucy*; second, to hear a few good songs from Richard Rodgers and Lorenz Hart, namely "I Didn't Know What Time It Was" and "You're Nearer." Interestingly enough, Ball's singing is dubbed by one Trudy Erwin.

## ☐ BACK IN THE SADDLE (1941)

This one you have to see just so you can say you watched the great singing cowboy Gene Autry in action, who eight years later bravely popularized "Rudolph the Red-Nosed Reindeer," when nobody else wanted anything to do with it. This little film features Autry singing the popular title tune as well as "You Are My Sunshine."

## ☐ THE BIG STORE (1941)

This is another typical Marx Brothers comedy, but it includes a more interesting array of songs, including "Tenement Symphony," "Sing While You Sell," "If It's You" (sung by Tony Martin), "Mamãe Eu Quero" (made famous by Carmen Miranda), Mozart's Piano Sonata no. 15 in C Major, K. 545 (Sonata semplice), and Beethoven's Minuet in G Major, WoO 10, no. 2 (played on the harp by Harpo Marx).

## ☐ BIRTH OF THE BLUES (1941)

Bing Crosby portrays a guy who grew up near Basin Street in New Orleans, playing his clarinet with the dockworkers. He puts together a band, and they struggle to get their jazz music accepted by the city's upper crust. Mary Martin joins them as a singer and gets Eddie "Rochester" Anderson to show her how to scat. It's all a reason to showcase some really good music and make clear the kind of prejudice white musicians encountered when they played the music of African Americans. In the film Crosby is actually referred to as "white trash" and asked why he likes this "darkie stuff." "Up till now folks never had Tabasco in their music," replies Crosby. "We're going to improve their taste." He performs the title tune as well as "Memphis Blues" by W. C. Handy,

"By the Light of the Silvery Moon," and "Tiger Rag." Martin sings "Cuddle Up a Little Closer, Lovey Mine" and "My Melancholy Baby." Together they sing "Wait Till the Sun Shines, Nellie." The movie is dedicated to "the musical pioneers of Memphis and New Orleans who favored the 'hot' over the 'sweet'— those early jazz men who took American music out of the rut and put it 'in the groove.'" Why moviemakers didn't have the nerve to really do that—instead of making caricatures of black musicians and actors—is a question best left to history scholars. Anderson rises above all this, as he does in so many films. This may be a whitewash, so to speak, of the origins of jazz, but it offers a lot of insight into the times. The film acknowledges the debt American music owes to African American musicians, whose work was imitated and stolen but perhaps never equaled. Watch for the jail scene in which the roots of jazz, pop, and the blues are rendered most vividly. Most DVDs of the film come with a set of extras that display authentic jitterbug and boogie-woogie. This film captures better than most the racial and ethnic segregation in America on the eve of World War II and early efforts to overcome it. The extraordinary title tune is effectively woven through the narrative.

☐ **BLUES IN THE NIGHT** (1941)

A fine example of film noir, this modest film stands out for tackling serious social issues, including the appropriation of musical styles from black Americans, crime, poverty, and abortion, all tied together with a strong plotline involving a penniless band dedicated to performing authentic blues music. Complications arise when the band hitches a ride in a boxcar and befriends a gangster. Priscilla Lane plays the singer with the band, and the score, including the unforgettable title song, is by Harold Arlen (music) and Johnny Mercer (lyrics). This movie is a real gem.

☐ **DUMBO** (1941) 🎬

This sometimes-underrated film has been called a tour de force in animation. The first ten minutes are almost continuous music, and it is believed to have inspired the creators of 2008's *WALL-E*. This movie is a treasure for the whole family.

☐ **LADY BE GOOD** (1941)

With "The Last Time I Saw Paris" and "You'll Never Know" to sing, Ann Sothern has never been in better form. Eleanor Powell dances up a storm in pro-

Robert Young and Ann Sothern in *Lady Be Good*

duction numbers, including the classic "Fascinating Rhythm," choreographed by the legendary Busby Berkeley. Robert Young (known later for television's *Father Knows Best* and *Marcus Welby, M.D.*) delivers in this serious story of success and its effect on a marriage. "Funny what a little success will do to you," says Lionel Barrymore as the judge in the divorce proceedings. Filmed in glorious black-and-white, the movie is typical of Hollywood in the 1940s, with its moral tone and conventional wisdom. Virginia O'Brien is briefly hilarious when singing "Your Words and My Music." Also interesting is an appearance by the Berry Brothers in a racially patronizing dance number— but they sure can dance! Eleanor Powell tapping her way through the title tune is the topper.

☐ **POT O' GOLD** (1941)

The great James Stewart and the lovely Paulette Goddard appear atypically in this fun musical about a music shop owner. It's an uncomplicated plot and a great example of Hollywood escapism on the verge of the United States entering World War II. Corny comedy is buttressed by memorable tunes like "A Knife, a Fork, and a Spoon" and "Hi, Cy, What's a-Cookin'?"

THE GREATEST GENERATION / 34

## ☐ THAT NIGHT IN RIO (1941)

To really appreciate this movie, you have to know what Carmen Miranda was up against. Constantly reduced to a stereotype, she nevertheless, fruit on her head, delivered irresistible tunes that made every American want to rush off to Brazil. "Chica Chica Boom Chic" opens the movie, and Don Ameche and Alice Faye then take over as the leads, Baron and Baroness Duarte. Ameche also plays a look-alike who adds to the silliness and allows him to sing a forgettable song to a fashion parade of beautiful women. The confusion that ensues gets sillier, but in the meantime, listen to a couple more of Miranda's best songs, "I Yi, Yi, Yi, Yi (I Like You Very Much)" and "Cai Cai."

## ☐ WEEK-END IN HAVANA (1941)

This movie doesn't lack talent; it's got the adorable Alice Faye, handsome Cesar Romero and John Payne, and fabulous Carmen Miranda. What it lacks is great songs. Made at a time when Cuba was still a glamorous destination for wealthy and famous Americans, the film cashes in on the contrast between old New York in winter and the warmth of the Caribbean. It all seems like a big fat cliché now, but in its time this kind of fun got people dancing, singing, and appreciating the rhythms of Latin America. You'll hear all sorts of references in Miranda's rendering of the title song. Who cares if she was from Brazil? It's interesting to note that one of the themes of the film hinges on a cruise ship going aground—sound familiar? The scenes filmed in Havana are a delight. Note that some DVDs of this film from the 20th Century Fox Marquee Musicals Collection contain audio commentary by film historian Jeanine Basinger, which helps to explain the conventions, styles, and techniques of this movie.

## ☐ YOU'LL NEVER GET RICH (1941)

When Rita Hayworth was paired to star in this film opposite the phenomenal Fred Astaire, there was speculation over whether or not the emerging star could match the superstar of dance. Hayworth proved herself to be one of the best dancing partners he ever had, Ginger Rogers notwithstanding. The exceptional dance scenes are reason enough to stick with the hokey plot to the end. There's "Boogie Barcarolle," "Shooting the Works for Uncle Sam," and "So Near and Yet So Far," all of which typify the swinging, patriotic 1940s. "The Wedding Cake Walk" is the best of boogie-woogie.

## ☐ ZIEGFELD GIRL (1941)

Judy Garland's transition to adult film star after *The Wizard of Oz* was complete by the end of this film, in which she plays a born-in-a-trunk vaudevillian trying to break away from her overly protective father and become a modern singer. She does it with two versions of "I'm Always Chasing Rainbows," a popular song based on a Chopin melody. Legendary innovator Busby Berkeley brings his imaginative camerawork and pacing to numbers that include Garland's calypso-infused "Minnie from Trinidad." Lana Turner and Hedy Lamarr star in the dramatic story line, with James Stewart as Turner's jilted boyfriend. Tony Martin sings "You Stepped Out of a Dream" beautifully, with Turner on one side and Lamarr on the other.

## ☐ FOOTLIGHT SERENADE (1942)

Betty Grable in boxing gloves—enough said. Favorite pin-up girl of GIs during World War II, she confirms in this film why her popularity somehow never resonated with me. This movie is filled with cloying, hyper song-and-dance numbers that hit you in the face like boxing gloves. Still, you must see this to believe it.

## ☐ FOR ME AND MY GAL (1942)

Direction by Busby Berkeley and a fine performance by Judy Garland, paired on film for the first time with Gene Kelly, make this melodramatic tale of a vaudeville song-and-dance duo that bucks through hard times and World War I on their way to success on Broadway. In addition to the title song, listen for "Oh, You Beautiful Doll," "After You've Gone," "Ballin' the Jack," and "When You Wore a Tulip and I Wore a Big Red Rose." Coming just three years after *The Wizard of Oz*, this movie shows how and why Garland established herself as a motion picture icon in adult roles that showcased her talent for comedy and drama, song and dance. The film features Marta Eggerth as Garland's bitchy competitor with the operatic voice, making the already beloved Judy even more appealing with her down-to-earth integrity.

## ☐ HOLIDAY INN (1942)

This film introduced the world to Irving Berlin's "White Christmas," with Bing Crosby singing it here as he does in the 1954 movie named for the song. Crosby's "White Christmas" has been the standard against which all

Bing Crosby, Fred Astaire, Marjorie Reynolds, and Virginia Dale in *Holiday Inn*

other versions have been measured. Featuring Crosby and Fred Astaire and directed by Mark Sandrich, this is a black-and-white classic that reflects the mores and styles of the 1940s.

### ☐ I MARRIED AN ANGEL (1942)

This whimsical black-and-white film marked the eighth and last film pairing of Jeanette MacDonald and Nelson Eddy. As the most eligible bachelor in Budapest, Count Palaffi grows weary of scheming women and dreams of a beautiful escape, a dream that yields opportunities to pair the count (Eddy) with a singing angel (MacDonald). The title tune is by Richard Rodgers and Lorenz Hart, who preceded Oscar Hammerstein II as Rodgers's writing partner. "I'll Tell the Man in the Street" is one of their best. "Tira Lira La (We're the Girls Who Want to Marry Willie)" is rather amusing, as the set is a costume party with wonderfully outlandish outfits on a bevy of babes, but one cannot miss the racist overtones in the off-putting treatment of the three little black children who are given a few brief lines in the number. Mostly this movie is a good example of how toned down so many film treatments of clever plays were because of the censorious Hays Code.

## ☐ MY GAL SAL (1942) 🎦

This biopic chronicles the life of songwriter Paul Dresser, played by Victor Mature, in the Gay Nineties, as he moves from carnival entertainer into New York society. Rita Hayworth stars and does the songs—dubbed by Nan Wynn.

## ☐ ORCHESTRA WIVES (1942)

Glenn Miller and his band feature prominently in this black-and-white fictional account filmed like a 1940s version of the reality of life on the road—it could have been called "Desperate Orchestra Wives." One reason for the reality factor is that Miller couldn't act his way out of a paper bag, but what a musician! Opening with the infectious "Chattanooga Choo Choo" and moving into "People like You and Me," "I've Got a Gal in Kalamazoo," and then on to the Nicholas Brothers dancing, it just doesn't get any better. You'd swear the Nicholas Brothers taught Fred Astaire and Gene Kelly everything they knew. This film delivers insight into the soundtrack of World War II and how it was when the beautiful song "At Last" first riveted young people to their jukeboxes. Trivia quiz: Recognize Jackie Gleason, Cesar Romero, and Harry Morgan?

## ☐ PANAMA HATTIE (1942)

The underappreciated Ann Sothern and Virginia O'Brien—not to mention music by Cole Porter—make this marginally important film a must-see. O'Brien's deadpan rendition of "Did I Get Stinkin' at the Club Savoy" (stinkin' drunk, that is) ais funny as all get out. The absolute highlights, however, are Lena Horne singing "Just One of Those Things" and the Berry Brothers (James, Nyas, and Warren) dancing to "Berry Me Not."

## ☐ PRESENTING LILY MARS (1942)

If you had not already fallen in love with the charms of Judy Garland by 1942, this film would have turned you around. She's adorable and all-American and all grown up, just three years away from *The Wizard of Oz*. This unpretentious black-and-white flick, costarring Van Heflin, is not so much a musical as a story with music. Marta Eggerth plays the anti-Garland and provides some beautiful (Russian-Ukrainian-Polish-whatever) operatic interludes, which seem slightly absurd. "Tom, Tom, the Piper's Son" is one of Garland's less known and cutest spots on film, and for the finale she does a great rendition of "Broadway Rhythm."

Bing Crosby, Dorothy Lamour, and Bob Hope in *Road to Morocco*

## ☐ PRIVATE BUCKAROO (1942)

The Andrews Sisters and Harry James and His Music Makers join the army and put on a camp show for the soldiers. Included are some great songs from the American songbook, including "You Made Me Love You," sung by Helen Forrest, and the Andrews Sisters' famous "Don't Sit under the Apple Tree (with Anyone Else but Me)." This film also helped make the Negro spiritual "Nobody Knows the Trouble I've Seen" more widely known to white audiences. Dick Foran singing "We've Got a Job to Do" followed by the Andrews Sisters performing "Johnny Get Your Gun Again" helped convince the nation that "we've got a war to be won."

## ☐ ROAD TO MOROCCO (1942) 🎞

You must watch at least one of the "Road" pictures that Bing Crosby and Bob Hope made together, and this one would be a good choice. It features a lot of music, most notably "Moonlight Becomes You," and it gives you some sense of the duo's appeal in these silly sexist capers. Dorothy Lamour had a lot to do with it, as the object of their desire, but I'll never forget going to the theater to see the last Road picture, *The Road to Hong Kong*, in 1962 and finding Lamour in a cameo role instead of the female lead. Apparently the guys considered her too old at forty-eight to be desirable; the lead went to Joan Collins.

## ☐ SONS OF THE PIONEERS (1942)

Although there was a tremendous growth of interest in Native American art and culture in the 1920s, by mid-century Hollywood movies and television had thoroughly sold cowboy heroes above Indians to the American public. Roy Rogers was probably the most popular of them all, with the possible exception of Gene Autry, who was really the first "singing cowboy." The influence these cowboys had on the baby boom generation cannot be underestimated. The point of these Westerns was that evil must triumph over good, and evil was not always "Injuns"; it was sometimes other cowboys. Sons of the Pioneers was also the name of a singing group that often backed Rogers on film. Although the plots and characters of Rogers's movies could be called clichés, they are also a lesson in ambition and courage. As a kid, I admired Roy Rogers and wondered how anyone could be that much larger than life. It was not until reading about him for this book that I learned his real name was Leonard Slye and he grew up near Portsmouth, Ohio.

★BEST *of the* BEST★

## ☐ YANKEE DOODLE DANDY (1942) 🎞️ 👤

This biographical musical is based loosely on the life of performing legend George M. Cohan, and, although it has subsequently been colorized, its splendor makes it hard to believe it was filmed in black-and-white. James Cagney, often typecast as a gangster, shows his true talent in this film with exuberant dancing and spectacular production numbers, and he won an Oscar for it. In addition to the title song, hear such classics as "Harrigan," "You're a Grand Old Flag," and "Give My Regards to Broadway."

James Cagney and Joan Leslie

☐ **YOU WERE NEVER LOVELIER** (1942)

Another film in glorious black-and-white, this is a moment when Rita Hayworth was never lovelier, and Fred Astaire tried the wings on his feet with dance partners other than Ginger Rogers. Xavier Cugat and His Orchestra provide a lot of the Latin-flavored music for Astaire's fancy footwork. A moonlight duet, "I'm Old Fashioned" by Jerome Kern and Johnny Mercer, is delightful.

☐ **BEST FOOT FORWARD** (1943)

A cadet at a military academy sends an invitation to movie star Lucille Ball to come to the big dance. Ball, playing herself in this film, is convinced to go in order to boost her career. Complications arise, offering opportunities to see the delightful June Allyson and Nancy Walker perform. A big bonus is getting to hear Harry James and His Music Makers play "Two O'Clock Jump" (a variation on the infectious "One O'Clock Jump" by Count Basie), "The Flight of the Bumblebee," and "My First Promise (The Ring Waltz)." Ball, who made her inability to sing a standing joke on her television show *I Love Lucy*, sings "You're Lucky," but don't be fooled. She is dubbed by Gloria Grafton.

☐ **CABIN IN THE SKY** (1943)

Never has a more beautiful torch song been sung on screen than "Happiness Is a Thing Called Joe," as rendered by Ethel Waters. Directed by the visionary Vincente Minnelli, this film defied racial conventions in America before the civil rights movement of the 1960s. It gives you a glimpse into the parallel universe that African Americans inhabited in a nation so racially divided that the equality promised by the abolition of slavery seemed like a dream that would never be fulfilled. Rising above all of this are Waters singing "Takin' a Chance on Love," Lena Horne singing "Honey in the Honeycomb," and Eddie "Rochester" Anderson singing "Life's Full o' Consequence." Lending fun to the film are Louis Armstrong, Butterfly McQueen (of *Gone with the Wind* fame) and Duke Ellington and His Orchestra, featuring swing dancing like you've never seen it.

☐ **DU BARRY WAS A LADY** (1943)

Notable not so much for the antics of its top-billed star, Red Skelton, as for the curious performance of Lucille Ball, who reveals not even a hint of the television comedy genius she became nearly a decade later. Her singing is clearly dubbed, while Gene Kelly, as the poor schmuck she says she truly loves, manages to deliver Cole Porter's "Do I Love You?" with enough gusto to make it the outstanding song in the film. Ignore the silly plot, which has Skelton becoming instantly rich and Ball agreeing to marry him for his money. The real stars of the film are Tommy Dorsey and His Orchestra delivering some solid jazz/swing with Gene Krupa on the drums, and the unforgettable Virginia O'Brien singing "Salome" and making Ball appear to have no comedic talent whatsoever.

## ☐ THE GANG'S ALL HERE (1943)

The hilarious Carmen Miranda is really the star of this movie, even though she is relegated, as she was for most of her Hollywood career, to a clown role, or as Edward Everett Horton calls her, a "South American savage." Her talent and wit rise above the script, as she sings "Brazil" and "Paducah." With America in the midst of World War II, this patriotic crumpet was directed by Busby Berkeley and features his trademark choreography during "The Lady in the Tutti Frutti Hat" and "The Polka-Dot Polka." Watch for the swing dancing as Benny Goodman sings "Minnie's in the Money," which makes *Dancing with the Stars* pale in comparison. Charlotte Greenwood's dance number is hilarious. Keep an eye out for the dancing Nicholas Brothers and Alice Faye singing the marginally memorable "A Journey to a Star."

## ☐ GIRL CRAZY (1943)

Mickey Rooney is at his exuberant best in this entertaining black-and-white romp with Judy Garland, featuring their renditions of some of the greats from the American songbook, including "Fascinating Rhythm," "Embraceable You," "But Not for Me," "Bidin' My Time," and "Could You Use Me?" George and Ira Gershwin wrote the music, Busby Berkeley choreographed, Tommy Dorsey and His Orchestra provided the accompaniment, and it doesn't get any better than that. Listen for the songs that will live beyond the movie. June Allyson and Nancy Walker are extremely amusing. Rooney's "Treat Me Rough" is daffy to this day. This is a very funny, joyful movie about values, befitting its wartime production.

## ☐ HELLO FRISCO, HELLO (1943)

A showcase for the vocal skills of Alice Faye singing "Ragtime Cowboy Joe," "Has Anybody Here Seen Kelly?" "By the Light of the Silvery Moon," "They Always Pick on Me" and the title tune, this film is an escapist romp into the music halls of San Francisco during the 1915 Panama Pacific Exhibition—at the height of World War II. But it's "You'll Never Know," one of the loveliest tunes of the twentieth century, that really raises this film to the top. The colorful costumes and sets are a treat, and there's music going almost every moment of the film. Corny as some of the numbers are—"It's Tulip Time in Holland" comes to mind—they are never dull. How can you be bored by a couple dozen Dutch boys and girls on wooden roller skates?

## ☐ STAGE DOOR CANTEEN (1943)
What I love about this black-and-white film is its earnestness and authenticity. Nearly seventy of Hollywood's biggest celebrities contributed their services to this wartime musical about the rocky romance between a soldier and a hostess at New York City's fabled USO canteen. Set to the big band music of Benny Goodman, Guy Lombardo, Kay Kyser, Xavier Cugat, and Count Basie, this memorable film features cameos of Katharine Hepburn, Ethel Merman, Ray Bolger, Gypsy Rose Lee, Harpo Marx, Peggy Lee, and countless others.

## ☐ STAR SPANGLED RHYTHM (1943)
Bing Crosby heads a Hollywood cast of "more stars than there are in the flag," as they sing and dance for the morale of the nation during World War II. You get to hear an awful lot of songs in the process, including "That Old Black Magic" and "Hit the Road to Dreamland" (sung by Dick Powell and Mary Martin, with the Golden Gate Quartet). Making appearances are the familiar faces of Betty Hutton, Dorothy Lamour, Veronica Lake, Paulette Goddard, Fred MacMurray, and Bob Hope doing an early stint entertaining the troops, a practice that became his hallmark through subsequent wars. Studio executives, such as Cecil B. DeMille, appear as themselves, and the corny plot and situations give some real insight into the mind-set of the viewing public at the time.

## ☐ STORMY WEATHER (1943) 🎞
There are two ways to look at this film with its all-black cast. One is with sadness that the assembly demonstrates how much musical talent went unheard and unseen by the mainstream in a country deeply divided along racial lines. The other is with gratitude that the movie ever got made and left us this invaluable record of life in a not-so-distant age. Bill "Bojangles" Robinson stars, in a role paralleling his own career, with Lena Horne and appearances by some of the most talented people in show business: Cab Calloway and His Cotton Club Orchestra, the one and only Fats Waller ("Ain't Misbehavin'"), Ada Brown, Katherine Dunham and her dancers, and the Nicholas Brothers,

Fayard and Harold. There are more than two dozen songs featured, and the dance sequences are top-notch, if you can get past the minstrel show stereotypes. Best remembered for his dance on the stairs with Shirley Temple in *The Little Colonel*, Robinson dances and mugs his way through the film as each act unfolds. I'm particularly fond of "I Lost My Sugar in Salt Lake City," as sung by Mae E. Johnson. Horne blows racial stereotypes away when she sings "I Can't Give You Anything but Love" in a duet with Robinson, and her rendition of the title song is a classic.

☐ **THANK YOUR LUCKY STARS** (1943)

If the appeal and popularity of Eddie Cantor have never made sense to you, this movie might change your mind. He has never been funnier and makes plenty of jokes at his own expense, especially as he is about to mistakenly

*Thank Your Lucky Stars* features a bevy of movie stars from Warner Bros. studios.

undergo a lobotomy! In addition to Cantor, the "stars" of the film's title refer to movie stars, and this film is packed with them—notably Dinah Shore, in probably her best film role. Olivia de Havilland and Ida Lupino make dubbed musical cameo appearances, as does the great Errol Flynn, who talks over his own dub track to tell the audience, "Oh, that voice is so divine. I'm sorry it isn't mine." Bette Davis is hilarious as she sings in her own voice "They're Either Too Young or Too Old." A surprisingly entertaining film.

### ☐ THIS IS THE ARMY (1943)

Here's another one of those World War II movies designed to rally the nation and boost morale. A message during the opening credits says that proceeds from the film would go to the United States Army Emergency Relief Fund. It's all a good excuse to put on a show so entertainers can do what they do best; here they get to do it with a slew of Irving Berlin songs, including "My Sweetie," sung and danced by George Murphy (who later became a U.S.

★ BEST *of the* BEST ★

### ☐ MEET ME IN ST. LOUIS (1944) 🎬

What makes this movie so durable is the way the ensemble works together to capture the flavor of an American age, as the family anticipates the 1904

Margaret O'Brien and Judy Garland

World's Fair. Even though this is clearly Judy Garland's movie, there are grand moments with every cast member as each moves the story along. The theme of home and what it means to have to leave it lingers from *The Wizard of Oz*, and little Margaret O'Brien as Tootie acts out her anger in ways that Dorothy would never have dreamed of. Then there are the songs, woven beautifully into the story line: "The Trolley Song," "The Boy Next Door," the title song, of course, and the saddest Christmas song ever written, "Have Yourself a Merry Little Christmas." This musical has never been equaled for laughs and tears all rolled up with song in one superior package, directed by none other than Vincente Minnelli.

senator); "God Bless America," belted out by the formidable Kate Smith; "What Does He Look Like?" sung by Frances Langford; and the title tune "This Is the Army Mr. Jones." Berlin himself sings "Oh! How I Hate to Get Up in the Morning" with the chorus. And watch for Ronald Reagan, future president of the United States, as he talks patriotism to his girlfriend, played by the all-American Joan Leslie. The patriotic message of this movie seems to have been pretty effective for at least two of its stars.

## ☐ CAN'T HELP SINGING (1944)

For insight into the enormous popularity of soprano singing sensation Deanna Durbin, who dropped out of films for good at age twenty-eight, this is a good bet. The music is some of the lesser-known work of Jerome Kern, and this is Durbin's only movie in Technicolor.

## ☐ COVER GIRL (1944)

With music by Jerome Kern and lyrics by Ira Gershwin, how can you go wrong? The film opens with the classic "Long Ago and Far Away" and never lets up as Gene Kelly and Rita Hayworth dance their way through this fine example of a 1940s Technicolor romp. This film is remembered as a turning point in the history of Hollywood musicals, because its songs were not merely strung together but were themselves vital elements in moving the story forward. Hayworth comes across as one of the most alluring women ever to appear on the silver screen—a term, by the way, that comes from the actual silver or aluminum embedded in the material that made up the reflective surface of early motion picture screens.

## ☐ FOLLOW THE BOYS (1944)

It seems to take forever to get through a plodding buildup, including a stiff performance by George Raft as a dancer, with ballerina Vera Zorina as his partner, but there is no better example of how Hollywood rallied to entertain the troops during World War II than this impressive parade of celebrities, showcasing some of the most popular acts of the time: Sophie Tucker talk-singing "The Better the Lovin' Will Be," the Andrews Sisters doing a string of their hits, Jeanette MacDonald singing "Beyond the Blue Horizon," Dinah Shore performing "I'll Walk Alone," and virtually the entire roster of contract actors at Universal Pictures appearing in one way or another. The footage of actual soldier audiences is nearly as interesting as the studio performances with which it is interspersed.

## ☐ **GOING MY WAY** (1944) 🎞️

Less a musical than a feel-good film about a younger Catholic priest, Bing Crosby, and a set-in-his-ways older priest played by Barry Fitzgerald. Opera singer Risë Stevens seems to have been cast in the film strictly to sing "Habanera" from *Carmen*. One memorable tune to listen for is "Swingin' on a Star."

## ☐ **HOLLYWOOD CANTEEN** (1944)

Warner Bros. used its star-making machinery to produce this film about a GI who drops in at the Hollywood Canteen during World War II hoping to meet his favorite movie star, Joan Leslie, a huge box office attraction at the time. From the opening song by the Andrews Sisters to the closing credits, this quintessential 1940s fare was buoyed by the contributions of dozens of movie stars (playing themselves). Jane Wyman (then married to Ronald Reagan) and Jack Carson sing "What Are You Doing the Rest of Your Life?" (fairly obviously dubbed), and my personal favorite, Cole Porter's "Don't Fence Me In," is sung by Roy Rogers and reprised by the Andrews Sisters after they sing that they are "Getting Corns for My Country" while dancing with GIs at the Hollywood Canteen. The inclusion of the Golden Gate Quartet singing "The General Jumped at Dawn" is an interesting comment on racial segregation in the military. And yes, our GI gets to meet Joan Leslie, and she gives him the sweetest screen kiss ever.

## ☐ **THOUSANDS CHEER** (1944)

Gene Kelly stars as a circus aerialist who reluctantly becomes a GI, then falls in love with the colonel's daughter, played by Kathryn Grayson, who decides to put on a mammoth show for the servicemen. This, of course, gives MGM studios an opportunity to round up a host of stars to perform in the show, among them Eleanor Powell dancing to "Boogie Woogie," Lena Horne singing "Honeysuckle Rose," and Judy Garland doing "The Joint Is Really Jumpin' in Carnegie Hall." Kelly shows off his dancing skills in "Let Me Call You Sweetheart," a duet with a mop, and Grayson raises her voice rather impressively in Verdi's "Sempre Libera," José Iturbi conducting. This movie gives you a sentimental sense of what the World War II years were like. The surprisingly likable "I Dug a Ditch" serves as an underlying theme song and is performed several times in the film with different arrangements. Grayson sings a version using an exaggerated "cowboy" accent, and Kelly dances to an instrumental version while partnering with a broom, having jilted the mop. The plot of this wartime film is strong and serves as more than a thread to hold the numbers together, but the comedy stylings of Mickey Rooney, Red Skelton, and Ben Blue might instigate the use of the fast-forward button on your remote control.

## ☐ TWO GIRLS AND A SAILOR (1944)

Charming Van Johnson plays a sailor caught between two sisters (played by June Allyson and Gloria DeHaven) to the rumba rhythms of Xavier Cugat and His Orchestra. This wartime film is another glimpse into what it took to keep "the boys" inspired. Among the song treats are "Sweet and Lovely"; "A-Tisket A-Tasket"; "Granada"; "Charmaine," performed by Harry James and His Music Makers; "Paper Doll," performed in a cameo by Lena Horne; "Inka Dinka Doo," done by Jimmy Durante; and "Ritual Fire Dance," played on the piano by José Iturbi.

## ☐ ANCHORS AWEIGH (1945)

With the famous José Iturbi leading the navy band in the title song, this paean to the men who serve gave Gene Kelly a chance to choreograph some great dance numbers, including his famous scene with Jerry, a cartoon mouse. This Technicolor musical comedy stars Kelly and Frank Sinatra as two sailors who go on a four-day shore leave in Hollywood. They meet an aspiring young singer, played by Kathryn Grayson, and try to help her get an audition at MGM. "If You Knew Susie (Like I Know Susie)" with Sinatra and Kelly is clever, but Kelly teaching Sinatra how to pick up women is really hilarious. Sinatra's version of "I Fall in Love Too Easily" and Iturbi's "The Donkey Serenade" were enormously popular in their time and are still worth listening to. Although her characters are not usually very warm or human, Grayson is quite lovable in this film, and she modulates her soprano beautifully for "(All of a Sudden) My Heart Sings."

## ☐ THE DOLLY SISTERS (1945) ▉

Betty Grable was considered quite the hot number in her day—a favorite pinup girl of American soldiers. I always thought she had a crabby look on her face. Be that as it may, this is one of her biggest hits, probably her most lavish musical, made at the peak of her career. An up-and-coming June Haver also stars. Although it has some basis in the lives of the real Dolly Sisters, the film makes no effort to be authentically biographical. It traces the rise and heart-

Betty Grable and June Haver in *The Dolly Sisters*

break of the sisters as they conquer vaudeville, Broadway, and Europe, singing tunes like "Carolina in the Morning," "Give Me the Moonlight, Give Me
the Girl," "I'm Always Chasing Rainbows," and the newer tune "I Can't Begin
to Tell You," which was a Hit Parade favorite. If you watch a copy that hasn't
been cut, the outrageous production numbers are considered the height of
kitsch today—"monuments to bad taste," as they have been called—that must
be seen to be believed. "The Darktown Strutters' Ball" features Grable and
Haver with bronzed faces, singing in mutilated French, and cavorting around
a Harlem set as pig-tailed "pickaninnies" surrounded by deeply tanned chorus girls in hats made of watermelons, dice, and playing cards. It's quite a
spectacle.

☐ **RHAPSODY IN BLUE** (1945) 📷

No doubt more fabrication than fact, this biopic with Robert Alda as the great
American songwriter George Gershwin contains some thirty of the composer's greatest hits and constitutes a musical education in one of the most
important chapters in the American songbook.

## ☐ STATE FAIR (1945)

One of the less appreciated musicals created by Richard Rodgers and Oscar Hammerstein II, *State Fair* has more than its "fair" share of their best songs, including "It Might as Well Be Spring" and "It's a Grand Night for Singing." The film idealizes and gently mocks rural life in Iowa. "I've got the most a woman can get in life; if I think any more about it, I'll cry," says Fay Bainter after taking the top prize for her mincemeat. Jeanne Crain stars as a bored girl with big dreams, longing to escape. "All I Owe Ioway" is a hoot, as we would say in the Midwest. The film was remade (but little improved) with Pat Boone and Ann-Margret in 1962 and is notable for the return to films of the great Alice Faye after nearly twenty years.

## ☐ YOLANDA AND THE THIEF (1945)

Fred Astaire plays a con man in a fictitious Latin American country who attempts to dupe a girl to get at her father's millions. Directed by Vincente Minnelli, the film is best remembered for its surrealistic "Dream Ballet" scene, with Astaire, costar Lucille Bremer, and others set against scenery reminiscent of the work of artist Salvador Dalí.

## ☐ BLUE SKIES (1946)

Bing Crosby was enormously popular over several decades, with a style that comes across as either smooth and debonair or smug and arrogant, depending on your taste. Here, he's paired with Fred Astaire, whose appeal as a dancer is obvious. With a retrospective of music and lyrics by Irving Berlin, this movie couldn't lose. "Puttin' on the Ritz" is one of the best Astaire dance numbers ever captured on film. Watch him twirl up a staircase during "A Pretty Girl Is like a Melody." The tunes just keep coming, one after another: "You'd Be Surprised," sung by adorable Olga San Juan, who gained fame briefly as the "Puerto Rican Pepperpot"; "All By Myself," sung by Crosby and costar Joan Caulfield; "C-U-B-A," with its interesting comment on Prohibition; "You Keep Coming Back like a Song"; "How Deep Is the Ocean?"; and, of course, the title song. "A Couple of Song and Dance Men" is a tour de force that Crosby and Astaire make look effortless, and "Heat Wave" is unbeatable. Billy De Wolfe's musical monologue as a lady is a must-see. This show could have been called "The Irving Berlin Review." For good measure, it even tacks on "White Christmas."

## ☐ HOLIDAY IN MEXICO (1946)

Featuring a very young Jane Powell and the great orchestra leader José Iturbi and bandleader Xavier Cugat, this film has so many great musical moments it's difficult to pick the best. The combination of classical music and Latin tunes plays through the story of a young girl's struggles with coming-of-age. Often underrated and seldom on the radar of lovers of musicals, it's time to bring this one out for family viewing time. The seventeen-year-old Powell singing "Ave Maria" with a full orchestra is as good as movie music gets.

## ☐ TWO SISTERS FROM BOSTON (1946)

A huge hit for MGM and Kathryn Grayson, the black-and-white film features a lot of classical music, Liszt and Wagner, among others, with Jimmy Durante for comic relief. The always fresh-as-a-daisy June Allyson plays the other sister and balances Grayson's rebellious side, as she defies her puritanical family and shows her limbs on a turn-of-the-century vaudeville stage. Grayson has never been funnier than when she is disrupting the opera sequence from *Lohengrin*, as the great Lauritz Melchior fumes his way through the aria. Musicals of this period may not be profound, but they are still a lot of fun to watch—in this case, especially when Melchior's dog hears "his master's voice" in a re-creation of the earliest recording session.

## ☐ ZIEGFELD FOLLIES (1946)

Portrayed by William Powell, the great theater impresario Florenz Ziegfeld (who died in 1932) looks down from heaven and ordains a new grand revue in his spectacular style, which offers a great excuse to show off much of the talent in the MGM studios. Among the outstanding specialty numbers: "Here's to the Girls," sung by Fred Astaire and danced by Cyd Charisse and Lucille Ball (of *I Love Lucy* fame) and a chorus of "cat women"; "Bring on the Wonderful Men," by the always hilarious Virginia O'Brien; "Love," performed by Lena Horne; "Limehouse Blues," danced by Astaire and Lucille Bremer; George Gershwin's "The Babbitt and the Bromide," sung and danced by Astaire and Gene Kelly; and "A Great Lady Has an Interview (Madame Crematante)," sung and danced by Judy Garland at her comic best, with an adoring male chorus exulting the invention of the safety pin.

## ☐ THE FABULOUS DORSEYS (1947) 🔳

This black-and-white film seems almost like a documentary, with legendary big band leaders Tommy and Jimmy Dorsey playing fictionalized versions of

## ☐ THE HARVEY GIRLS (1946)

This musical seldom makes anybody's top-ten list, but it is perfect in almost every way, except for the sappy ending in which Judy Garland and John Hodiak fall for each other, literally, and also fall almost completely out of character. Not only is the movie full of romantic songs, it is also funny as all get out. Watch Virginia O'Brien teach a queasy Ray Bolger to shoe a horse as she sings about "The Wild, Wild West." "Swing Your Partner Round and Round" showcases the comedic skills of Chill Wills and Marjorie Main. Angela Lansbury (who has one of the most durable careers in show business history) is delightful as the tough bordello madam with a heart of gold, singing "Oh, You Kid." This is a perfect antidote to the serious film Westerns that assert guns

Angela Lansbury

tamed the West, whereas this film makes a convincing case for classy waitresses. Garland's scene with a pair of six-shooters shows her gift for comedy and her ability to switch to romance in a flash. My particular favorite is "It's a Great Big World," sung by the dancing trio of Garland, O'Brien, and Cyd Charisse. The Oscar-winning "On the Atchison, Topeka and the Santa Fe" is one of Garland's finest moments on the silver screen. On YouTube, you can watch her singing "March of the Dogies"; this scene was cut from the film and is far better than many songs left in most movies.

themselves and delivering many of the hits that made them famous, including "Green Eyes," "I'm Getting Sentimental over You," and "Marie." Performances by big band musicians and singers from the 1940s, including Art Tatum, Charlie Barnet, Bob Eberly, Paul Whiteman, and Helen O'Connell help convey a sense of why this music is such a perfect expression of the American generation that won World War II with its determination and cockeyed optimism.

## ☐ THE PIRATE (1948)

Often taken far too seriously and therefore dismissed as a flop, this movie is instead a wildly funny spoof of pirate adventure fantasies, in which Judy

Gene Kelly and Judy Garland

Garland and costar Gene Kelly fall out of character regularly, all in the name of fun. It's almost like watching a series of skits on *The Carol Burnett Show,* way ahead of their time. It is also one of the only Garland films in which the highlights really belong to someone else: Kelly and, at one point, the Nicholas Brothers, for their dancing. The best dance number Kelly has ever recorded on film is his phenomenally athletic solo to "Mack the Black," not to mention his pole dance to "Niña." Gladys Cooper and Walter Slezak are hilarious without ever singing a note. "Be a Clown" is the absurd, totally unbelievable and utterly wonderful concluding number. Directed by Vincente Minnelli and ostensibly set on a nineteenth-century Caribbean island, this tongue-in-cheek tale is 1948 U.S.A. through and through, and it gets funnier with each viewing. "Aren't you interested in love?" Kelly teases. "No," Garland says emphatically, "I told you I was going to be married." This is one of the funniest movies I have ever seen.

## ☐ GOOD NEWS (1947)

In the Roaring Twenties at a fictitious university, coed and school librarian Connie Lane falls for football hero Tommy Marlowe. Unfortunately, he has his eye on gold-digging vamp Pat McClellan. It's all an excuse to watch vivacious June Allyson and suave Peter Lawford, along with brilliant Broadway dancer Joan McCracken, deliver tunes such as the title song and the wonderful "The Best Things in Life Are Free." The velvet voice of Mel Tormé delivers "Lucky in Love," and the "Varsity Drag" dance sequence is enough to get you on your feet!

## ☐ THE JOLSON STORY (1947) 

Larry Parks plays vaudeville and early film legend Al Jolson, but he has a hard time conveying the enormous appeal of the showbiz wonder who made a name for himself in blackface singing sappy versions of songs drawn from the Old South. Jolson's own voice is used to dub Parks, and this film brought him renewed popularity as he continued to influence other entertainers, from Judy Garland to Bob Dylan. A sequel to this film came out in 1950, *Jolson Sings Again.*

☐ **TILL THE CLOUDS ROLL BY** (1947) 🔳
Robert Walker plays Jerome Kern, the man who wrote *Show Boat* and many songs in the great American songbook. His life and times are brought to the screen by Walker along with Judy Garland playing Ziegfeld star Marilyn Miller and a host of stars presenting one musical treat after another. It's a great introduction to Kern's magnificent body of work. It opens with several numbers from *Show Boat*: Kathryn Grayson and Tony Martin sing "Make Believe"; Virginia O'Brien sings "Life Upon the Wicked Stage"; Lena Horne does "Can't Help Lovin' Dat Man"; and Caleb Peterson sings "Ol' Man River." Angela Lansbury does "How'd You Like to Spoon with Me," and Dinah Shore sings "They Didn't Believe Me" and "The Last Time I Saw Paris," while Garland sings "Look for the Silver Lining," "Sunny," and "Who." Cyd Charisse and Gower Champion dance to "Smoke Gets in Your Eyes," and the title song is a beautiful singin' and dancin' in the rain piece with June Allyson and Ray McDonald. Frank Sinatra (at the height of his popularity as a teen idol) reprises "Ol' Man River" (of all things!) for an unusual grand finale.

☐ **A DATE WITH JUDY** (1948)
Developed from a radio program that began in 1941, this vehicle for Jane Powell showcases her youthful energy, not to mention her glorious voice. The plot has Powell suffocated by her overly proper parents, pestered by her brother, and irritated by her boyfriend. This gives her an opportunity to sing "It's a Most Unusual Day" and "Love Is Where You Find It." Another reason to see this film is to see Elizabeth Taylor in an adolescent role.

☐ **EASTER PARADE** (1948)
Ann Miller's tap dance to "Shakin' the Blues Away" could be the best scene this superb dancer ever left on film. Like all the numbers in this sunny love story, it helps advance the plot, in which Fred Astaire is a dancer on the rebound from Miller, who makes a star out of Judy Garland—following a few blunders along the way. With the music and lyrics of master songwriter Irving Berlin, Garland has never been funnier, especially as she and Astaire mock high

society as "A Couple of Swells," singing the song while dressed as bums with dirty faces. The 1912 costumes and sets are really fun, especially the millinery fashion parade that opens the film. Astaire's tap dance in a toy store is a joy to watch. As a kid growing up on a farm in Michigan, I wasn't sure what to make of Judy Garland singing that paean to farm life, "I Want to Go Back to Michigan," just as I was beginning to dream about leaving it.

## ☐ ROMANCE ON THE HIGH SEAS (1948)

Doris Day makes her film debut as a wisecracking penniless singer who gets embroiled in a husband-wife jealousy caper and ends up impersonating the wife on a sea cruise. Mistaken identity and unlikely plot twists make this a screwball comedy with the added treats of Day singing "Throw 'Em in the Deep Blue Sea" and the beautiful signature song "It's Magic." It's Doris Day as you've never seen her or, more to the point, as you will never see her again. The music is by the highly successful writing team of Jule Styne and Sammy Cahn. Starring in nonsinging roles are the versatile Jack Carson, Janis Paige, Don DeFore, and everyone's favorite uncle in the 1940s, S. Z. Sakall. Avon Long, an African American Broadway performer, sings "The Tourist Trade," and pianist Oscar Levant shines on "Brazilian Rhapsody."

## ☐ WORDS AND MUSIC (1948) 📷

This is a spectacular musical, packed with the beloved hits of the famed song-writing team of Richard Rodgers and Lorenz Hart—before Rodgers went on to even greater things teamed with Oscar Hammerstein II. With Mickey Rooney as Hart and Tom Drake as Rodgers, we learn their story, laced with their greatest hits performed by the biggest stars of the day: "The Lady Is a Tramp" and "Where or When," performed by Lena Horne; "Manhattan," sung by Rooney and Drake; and "I Wish I Were in Love Again," performed by Rooney and Judy Garland (their last screen appearance together). Garland's rendition of "Johnny One Note" is a showstopper, as is "This Can't Be Love," danced by Cyd Charisse and Dee Turnell with ballerinas. Perry Como delivers "Mountain Greenery," "Blue Room," and "With a Song in My Heart," while Mel Tormé's version of "Blue Moon" is a classic. For me, however, *Slaughter on Tenth Avenue* was the real revelation in this film (though it made its debut in the Broadway production *On Your Toes* in 1936). Danced by Gene Kelly and Vera-Ellen and performed by the MGM Symphony Orchestra conducted by Lennie Hayton, this passionate and sophisticated mini-ballet is as mesmerizing today as it was more than half a century ago. There's not a move that isn't perfect, and the music is divine.

## ☐ THE BARKLEYS OF BROADWAY (1949)
The last movie Fred Astaire and Ginger Rogers made together is loaded with music by Harry Warren and lyrics by Ira Gershwin, including "They Can't Take That Away from Me," "Swing Trot," "You'd Be Hard to Replace," and "Manhattan Downbeat." It's thrilling to see Rogers, after you've seen a few of her earlier musicals, prove that she's an actress with her heartfelt recitation of "La Marseillaise" in French!

## ☐ IN THE GOOD OLD SUMMERTIME (1949)
Judy Garland and Van Johnson star in this pleasant turn-of-the-twentieth-century love story with great Americana in the score. Favorite song: "I Don't Care." Despite the title, this is a good one to pull out at Christmastime. Watch closely to the very end and you will see the screen debut of Garland's baby daughter, Liza Minnelli.

## ☐ THE KISSING BANDIT (1949)
Frank Sinatra and Kathryn Grayson star in this musical caper, with "Love Is Where You Find It," "Tomorrow Means Romance," "What's Wrong with Me?" and "I Steal a Kiss" among the notable numbers. But the real show-stealer is the hilarious "Dance of Fury," in which brilliant dancers Cyd Charisse and Ann Miller fight over dancing Latin lover Ricardo Montalban.

## ☐ MY DREAM IS YOURS (1949)
This musical comedy starring Doris Day is best remembered for the dream sequence combining animation and live action—Bugs Bunny gets to dance with Day and costar Jack Carson to the tune of the Hungarian Rhapsody no. 2. The title song sticks with you as well.

## ☐ NEPTUNE'S DAUGHTER (1949)
The best reason to watch an Esther Williams movie is to see the lavish production numbers built around the swimming champion taking a dip. Unable to compete in the 1940 Olympics because of the outbreak of World War II, Williams became a movie star instead—or perhaps earlier than expected. This film is one of her most enjoyable, especially because of her duet with

Ricardo Montalban on the Oscar-winning "Baby, It's Cold Outside," the cutest seduction number ever. If you remember Montalban as the Star Trek character Khan, you'll enjoy seeing him in his youth as a sexy young playboy with a very pleasant singing voice.

### ☐ ON THE TOWN (1949)

This adaptation of a Broadway play broke ground for filming on location in New York City instead of on a Hollywood set. A "torrent of talent and tunes," according to its promoters, the film focuses on the adventures of three sailors on the town for a twenty-four-hour shore leave. The team of Adolph Green and Betty Comden wrote the screenplay, with a young Leonard Bernstein composing some of the music. "New York, New York" is the catchy melody that infuses the entire film. The scenes with Vera-Ellen early in the movie are a precursor to similar scenes in *Gigi* with Leslie Caron. The whole movie is a preview of things to come and the last of the great World War II films. "What are you doin' drivin' a cab? The war's over," says Frank Sinatra to Betty Garrett, who decides on the spot that he's the guy for her. Gene Kelly, Ann Miller, and Jules Munshin round out the exuberant cast.

### ☐ TAKE ME OUT TO THE BALL GAME (1949)

An Esther Williams movie with no swimming! And she is delightful as the savvy female owner of a baseball team in the early days of the sport. Frank Sinatra, Gene Kelly, Betty Garrett, and Jules Munshin keep the fun coming, even as a crook threatens the team. Busby Berkeley directed this frisky romp that includes, of course, the title song, the hilarious "O'Brien to Ryan to Goldberg," and a closing number completely outside the plot, "Strictly U.S.A."

# ENTER THE
# GOLDEN AGE

Cinemascope, Technicolor, and the Advent of Television

**1950s**

A FTER WORLD WAR II, WITH THE ARRIVAL OF THE McCarthy era and communist paranoia, Hollywood was under siege, and competition from television led to bigger and more splendid and colorful productions and techniques, including Cinemascope, to draw audiences into movie theaters. Studios either made musicals super-American or took the location outside the United States, yet this pressure resulted in more of the greatest movie musicals than any other decade: *An American in Paris, Gigi, Brigadoon, South Pacific,* and *The King and I* among them, taking Americans to France, Scotland, Polynesia, and Siam (as Thailand was then known).

Other great films from this period looked to another time to avoid the here and now, notably *Singin' in the Rain,* which is set in the 1920s and gets lots of laughs over the transition of movies from silent to talkie. *The Band Wagon,* another great film from this period, picks up on this same difficulty and features Fred Astaire as a washed-up movie star looking to Broadway for a comeback, while *Guys and Dolls* fantasizes about gangsters of an earlier era. The hilarious *Calamity Jane* looks even farther back in film history as it makes fun of the conventions of movie Westerns. *Seven Brides for Seven Brothers* and *Oklahoma!* take a more romanticized look at the Old West but are still clearly in the realm of fantasy. *Damn Yankees* took the super-American sport of baseball and made it something to sing about, albeit in relation to saving one's soul.

The exception to the rule in the early 1950s was *A Star Is Born*, in which Judy Garland gives probably her best screen performance as a successful actress married to a washed-up actor drowning in alcohol. Although an ambitious film, it is completely apolitical. Other great films tackle more serious contemporary themes: *The Pajama Game*, in which all-American Doris Day plays a labor union representative, and *Porgy and Bess*, with its unflinching statements about racism and the undeniable American social conditions that resulted from slavery and segregation.

## ☐ ANNIE GET YOUR GUN (1950) 🎞

Music and lyrics by Irving Berlin make this one of the most successful musicals ever, but one wonders what this movie would have been like if Judy Garland had played sharpshooter Annie Oakley, as planned. It's hard to imagine that it would have gone well, but Garland certainly had the voice that Betty Hutton lacked. Still, Hutton is often quite amusing in this film, especially in the early scenes when she hams it up as a yokel singing "Doin' What Comes Natur'lly" and "You Can't Get a Man with a Gun." "I could shoot the fuzz off a peach," she brags, and her vocal duel with Howard Keel on "Anything You Can Do, I Can Do Better" is the high point of the film. All through the movie, as soon as one great song is over, another begins, from "There's No Business like Show Business" to "They Say It's Wonderful" to "I Got the Sun in the Morning." The portrayal of American Indians is really disconcerting—until one remembers that the film is based on the late-nineteenth-century touring spectacle called Buffalo Bill's Wild West, which actually employed members of the Sioux tribe, including Sitting Bull, as showbiz novelties. Nevertheless, Hutton singing "I'm an Indian Too" is just embarrassing.

## ☐ CINDERELLA (1950) 🎬

This animated version of the classic rags-to-riches story features the delightful "Bibbidi-Bobbidi-Boo," as the fairy godmother magically prepares Cinderella for the ball that will change her life. A family classic that is fun to watch over and over.

Louis Calhern, Betty Hutton, and Howard Keel in *Annie Get Your Gun*

### ☐ SUMMER STOCK (1950)

A latter-day spin on the "let's put on a show in the barn" theme of earlier Judy Garland movies, this one pairs her with Gene Kelly in a rivalry with her sister, played by Gloria DeHaven. It's all a little thin on plot, but Garland shines doing one of her classics, "Get Happy."

### ☐ TEA FOR TWO (1950)

In this reworking of the stage hit *No! No! Nanette!*, a wealthy heiress, played by the incomparable Doris Day, bets her uncle $25,000 that she can say no to everything for forty-eight hours. If she wins, he'll let her invest the money in a Broadway show—written by her beau, Gordon MacRae—in which she will star. Trouble is, she doesn't realize her uncle's just been wiped out by the stock market crash. The plot is, of course, a premise for Day and MacRae to sing such unforgettable tunes as "I Want to Be Happy," "Charleston," "I Know

That You Know," "Crazy Rhythm," "I Only Have Eyes for You," George and Ira Gershwin's "Do, Do, Do," and the unforgettable title tune.

## ☐ THREE LITTLE WORDS (1950) ▣

Fred Astaire must have been the busiest actor in Hollywood, popping up as he did in so many films. This time he costars with Red Skelton in one of Skelton's least obnoxious roles. This is the biographically based story of the songwriting team of Bert Kalmar and Harry Ruby, whose best-known songs are showcased in this film under the direction of André Previn, including "I Wanna Be Loved by You," "Nevertheless," and "Who's Sorry Now?" The movie features the incredible dancer Vera-Ellen, a young Debbie Reynolds, and the lovely Arlene Dahl. Watch for "Mr. and Mrs. Hoofer at Home," in which Astaire and Vera-Ellen demonstrate what happens when two dancers get married.

## ☐ YOUNG MAN WITH A HORN (1950)

What a stupendous soundtrack this drama boasts. More film noir than musical, the movie belongs to Kirk Douglas as Rick Martin, the young man who lives for his music. Doris Day costars in her first dramatic role as his friend (who's in love with him), and Lauren Bacall plays her friend (with whom he is in love). More than an excuse to put beautiful songs and dancing on the screen, this is a compelling story about music and the price of devotion to it. Rick and his mentor, played by Juano Hernandez, make the difference between European music and original American music abundantly clear. Hernandez is an underrated Hollywood phenomenon who broke new ground for black actors in 1949, when he acted in his first mainstream film based on William Faulkner's novel *Intruder in the Dust*. Orley Lindgren plays Rick as a boy, and anybody who longs for "the good old days" needs to see the early scenes of this movie for a rude awakening. The score is superb, with the legendary Hoagy Carmichael as the narrator who takes you into the smoke-filled world of jazz in 1950. The great trumpeter Harry James dubs for Douglas on "Shadow Waltz" and accompanies Day as she sings "The Very Thought of You" as it's never been sung before or since. A jazzed-up version of "Get Happy" by Carmichael and James is a pivotal scene, as is Day's rendition of "Too Marvelous for Words" and "With a Song in My Heart." If you are not in love with Doris Day, you will be after this film, especially after a neurotic Bacall says, "She's so terribly normal."

★BEST *of the* BEST★

## ☐ AN AMERICAN IN PARIS (1951) ▨

The most enduring of all the great musicals Vincente Minnelli (or anybody else) directed, this soaring production pairs Gene Kelly with Leslie Caron in Paris after World War II. The songs are by George and Ira Gershwin and each one is a classic—"I Got Rhythm," "Embraceable You," "Our Love Is Here to Stay," "'s Wonderful," "Stairway to Paradise." Some critics dislike the seventeen-minute ballet that Kelly and Caron dance in the middle of the film. I watch it over and over and continue to find it a miracle of choreography (Kelly's). My only misgiving about the film is the casting of Georges Guétary as Caron's older lover; he was actually three years younger than Kelly and looks it.

Gene Kelly and Leslie Caron

The unrelentingly cynical piano player Oscar Levant redeems himself in this film with "By Strauss," which features old women dancing with delight, and Kelly singing with the children about "le bubble gum" is watchable over and over again. But this is not a movie for children; the story, after all, is about an aspiring artist who is using a wealthy American heiress to get ahead, while wooing a young girl who is engaged—to his dear friend, as it turns out. This is the movie that made me fall in love with Paris, and every time I watch it I see something new. Last time, I took Nina Foch's side and got a new view of Kelly's character. He's quite the little user, to put it politely. Try it after you've seen the film a couple of times. Then watch *Singin' in the Rain* again and take Jean Hagen's side as she plays Lina Lamont trying to hang on to her career. Once you wise up to Debbie Reynolds as scheming Kathy, it's like watching the movie for the first time!

## ☐ THE GREAT CARUSO (1951) ▨

Another musical from MGM, this one is probably Mario Lanza's best film and one of the most interesting film biographies ever. Watch this film knowing that Mario Lanza contributed significantly to making opera more popular in America. Here he portrays the great opera star Enrico Caruso. This film is so Italian, so Catholic, it will amaze you that it got made in the 1950s; and how can you not marvel at that voice? Bonus: There are echoes of this film more than forty years later in *Evita*, especially at the beginning, when Caruso's mother dies. Mario Lanza was a phenomenal success for a short time, but he left a film legacy worth learning about.

### ☐ ON MOONLIGHT BAY (1951)

Set at the time of World War I but released during the Korean War, this Doris Day–Gordon MacRae delight is designed to fire up your patriotism and family values—a great movie for the Fourth of July. In the process, you get to hear some sappy, silly, and thoroughly singable songs. I am convinced that seeing this movie once when I was very young turned me on to songs that I still know almost all the words to more than a half a century later: "Moonlight Bay," "I'm Forever Blowing Bubbles," "Pack Up Your Troubles in Your Old Kit Bag and Smile, Smile, Smile!" "Cuddle Up a Little Closer, Lovey Mine," "Till We Meet Again," "Ain't We Got Fun," and "Oh, You Beautiful Doll." This film was so popular that Warner Bros. immediately filmed *By the Light of the Silvery Moon*, a sequel with all the actors playing the same characters, an unusual thing for a studio to do at the time.

### ☐ ROYAL WEDDING (1951)

Best remembered for Fred Astaire dancing on the ceiling and with a coat rack, this film pairs Astaire with the young Jane Powell as a brother and sister act in London during the wedding of Princess Elizabeth and Prince Philip. With music by Burton Lane and lyrics by Alan Jay Lerner, the story echoes the real-life theatrical relationship of Fred and Adele Astaire. Powell is surprisingly able to keep up with Astaire in every way, and her singing voice is superb as she sails through "Happiest Day of My Life" and "Too Late Now." "How Could You Believe Me When I Said I Love You When You Know I've Been a Liar All My Life" is a scream.

### ☐ SHOW BOAT (1951)

Just fifteen years after the 1936 film version of *Show Boat,* starring Irene Dunne, the wildly successful musical was made into a Technicolor, razzle-dazzle spectacle starring Kathryn Grayson, Ava Gardner (whose voice was dubbed), and Howard Keel. The Jerome Kern songs are as beautiful as ever, including the immortal "Make Believe" and "Can't Help Lovin' Dat Man." Gorgeous as the film is, it does not gloss over the reality of the American racial divide, when integration and miscegenation were prohibited by law. This musical is the one that changed American musical theater from light comedy to near opera. William Warfield's rendition of "Ol' Man River" is as wise and sad a song as has ever been sung in the history of America. Tip: See the 1936 version first.

☐ **THE BELLE OF NEW YORK** (1952)
Set in New York circa 1900, this box office failure nevertheless features two of the best dancers ever filmed, Fred Astaire and Vera-Ellen, with music by Harry Warren and lyrics by the one and only Johnny Mercer. It's virtuous Bowery

---

★ BEST *of the* BEST ★

☐ **SINGIN' IN THE RAIN** (1952) 🎞
This classic romp often tops critics' and audiences' lists of best musicals—sometimes of best movies, period—of all time. Gene Kelly and Donald O'Connor star as dancing bud-

dies, while Debbie Reynolds sets her sights on Kelly by trying to convince him that she is not the least bit interested. Watch as O'Connor throws himself around like a rag doll, singing "Make 'Em Laugh." Cyd Charisse, one of the best dancers ever to appear on screen, adds elegance to a film that is set in the 1920s, when sound motion pictures spelled the end for many a whiney-voiced silent film star, as spoofed in this

Gene Kelly

film by the hilarious Jean Hagen. The film also revived the song of the same title by Nacio Herb Brown and Arthur Freed, which was first popularized in *Hollywood Revue of 1929*. Gene Kelly and Stanley Donen directed the movie, with story and screenplay by the dynamic husband-and-wife team Betty Comden and Adolph Green. What a glorious feeling; I'm happy again.

mission worker versus wealthy playboy, with his carefree days brought to an end when he falls in love. While trying to resolve their differences, the stars perform dazzling dance routines, one of which was inspired by Currier and Ives art. Vera-Ellen's "Naughty but Nice" steams, and Astaire's "I Wanna Be a Dancin' Man" is a knockout. My nomination for a movie line ahead of its time is Fred Astaire explaining his need to earn Vera-Ellen's attention by doing honest work: "It's the uptrodden who need saving these days."

### ☐ HANS CHRISTIAN ANDERSEN (1952) 🔳

A toned-down Danny Kaye stars in this "once upon a time" fairy tale about the greatest fairy tale spinner of all, Denmark's Hans Christian Andersen, creator of "The Little Mermaid." Music and lyrics by Frank Loesser yield some memorable tunes, my favorite being "Inchworm," sung by Kaye and the children in the film. There are many songs featured, with "Wonderful Copenhagen," "Thumbelina," "Anywhere I Wander," and "No Two People" well worth listening to and singing again and again. The lovely "Little Mermaid Ballet" is based on Franz Liszt's B Minor Piano Sonata (1854), *Les préludes* (1856), *Tasso* (1849), and a Mephisto waltz, and is performed by Zizi Jeanmaire, Roland Petit, and the Roland Petit Ballet. This is an often underestimated and neglected film.

### ☐ STARS AND STRIPES FOREVER (1952) 🔳

Clifton Webb stars in this film biography of the composer John Philip Sousa, from his early days in the Marine Corps Band through the Spanish-American War in 1898. It may surprise you how familiar many of the tunes in this film are—and how patriotic you may feel when you hear them.

### ☐ WHERE'S CHARLEY? (1952)

What fun to watch and listen as the marvelous Ray Bolger (the scarecrow in *The Wizard of Oz*) sings and dances to "Once in Love with Amy." The film was based on a Broadway hit that garnered Bolger a Tony Award, but it's very hard to find a copy of this film to watch at home, since (as of this writing) it has not been released on video or DVD, and it was last broadcast on television in the 1970s. Let's hope it is safely archived somewhere; meanwhile, you can watch snippets on YouTube.

★BEST *of the* BEST★

## ☐ THE BAND WAGON (1953)

Another of the outstanding musicals directed by Vincente Minnelli, *The Band Wagon* often appears on lists of greats, and it is the perfect vehicle for the talents of Fred Astaire. I've always marveled at how this skinny weak-voiced guy with the bony face and eternally receding hairline could be such a matinee idol. The film examines this phenomenon, casting Astaire as a washed-up movie star looking for a comeback. Although Astaire does not have a great singing voice, he has an appealing one, and he pulls off "By Myself" and "Dancing in the Dark" with elegance and style. He's mesmerizing. It is also interesting to note that in racist

Fred Astaire and Cyd Charisse

America, Minnelli's films always included black folks, as in Astaire's duet with Leroy Daniels during "A Shine on Your Shoes." And "That's Entertainment" has got to be the best showbiz song ever premiered in a film. Oscar Levant, Nanette Fabray, and Jack Buchanan lend just the right amount of oddness to the film, especially when the latter two sing "Triplets" with Astaire, dressed as infants. In their duet "Dancing in the Dark," Astaire and Cyd Charisse make it all look so easy, but you'll never see anything better than this on film.

## ☐ WITH A SONG IN MY HEART (1952)

Call it melodrama, but Susan Hayward turns in a major performance as singer Jane Froman, who leaves on a European tour but loses her legs when her plane crashes in Lisbon. Nevertheless, she goes on to entertain the Allied troops during World War II. Hayward's voice is dubbed by the real Jane Froman, as she sings a slew of classic tunes, including the great title song and "That Old Feeling," "Get Happy," "Blue Moon," "Home on the Range," "Embraceable You," "Tea for Two," "It's a Good Day," "They're Either Too Young or Too Old," "I'll Walk Alone," "America the Beautiful," "Give My Regards to Broadway,"

## ☐ CALAMITY JANE (1953)

Doris Day gives her funniest performance in this farce based on the life of a real frontier character. From the "Deadwood Stage" opening to the delightful "Secret Love" closing, Day pulls off this satire better than anyone else could have, and if you've just seen *Annie Get Your Gun*, you will wonder why Betty Hutton got that role. Day is pitch-perfect as Calamity Jane, especially in the early part of the film when she is the butch cowgirl, before she gets a feminine makeover and snares her shooting buddy (Howard Keel, in fine voice). The problem with this movie for a contemporary audience is the portrayal of "Injuns" as good candidates for target practice. But the cowboys are treated with equal disrespect, as Day regularly calls them names like "pagan varmint" or "toothless old buffalo"—to their faces. It's great fun to see how this movie plays with gender. When a case of mistaken identity forces Dick Wesson to dress up as a woman to entertain the boys in the saloon, they begin to suspect that he is not the real Adelaid Adams, as billed. "That ain't all she ain't," quips Day under her breath. "I Can Do without You" and "Just Blew in from the Windy City" are numbers that showcase not only Doris Day's beautiful voice but also her athletic dancing, as she leaps on top of the bar and challenges any of the boys to mess with her.

Doris Day

"Chicago," "California Here I Come," "Carry Me Back to Old Virginny," "Alabamy Bound," "Deep in the Heart of Texas," and "Dixie."

## ☐ CALL ME MADAM (1953)

Watch this film for two insights into American musicals. First is an appreciation of just how marvelous, too marvelous for words, the music of Irving Berlin is and why it captured the American imagination so rapturously. Second is the dynamism of Ethel Merman, who sang her way to popularity on Broadway and was often relegated to second fiddle on screen. This movie, silly as the plot is, serves as a showcase for Merman's vocal and comic skills.

It's filled with Berlin favorites like "The Hostess with the Mostes' on the Ball," "It's a Lovely Day Today," and the terrific duet between Donald O'Connor and Merman, "You're Just in Love." Watch for the marvelous dance sequence by O'Connor, best known for *Singin' in the Rain*, and Vera-Ellen, most often remembered for *White Christmas*.

## ☐ DANGEROUS WHEN WET (1953)

Among the most charming of swimming star Esther Williams's films, this one features a scene in which she swims with cartoon cat and mouse Tom and Jerry. The score is quite easy on the ear, and it's interesting to note that Williams met her costar, Fernando Lamas, on the set of this film and later married him.

## ☐ GENTLEMEN PREFER BLONDES (1953)

Marilyn Monroe makes the most of her weak singing voice and her much stronger physical attributes in this strangely adorable musical comedy. She and Jane Russell play latter-day gold diggers, small-town lounge singers determined to make the most of their assets on a cruise to Paris. As obvious as they are, the men are taken in, and the gals get to sing some songs from the Broadway show on which the movie is based that really stick in your craw, mostly those written by Jule Styne and Leo Robin: "Two Little Girls from Little Rock," "Diamonds Are a Girl's Best Friend," and "Bye Bye Baby." For real laughs, check out "Anyone Here for Love?" performed by a tough-talking Russell surrounded by exercising athletes from the 1952 U.S. Olympic Team. Monroe as Lorelei Lee defined the proverbial "dumb blonde" for generations to come—dumb like a fox!

## ☐ KISS ME KATE (1953)

Kathryn Grayson and Howard Keel play a divorced pair of actors who are brought together by Cole Porter, who has written a musical version of Shakespeare's *The Taming of the Shrew*. Of course, the two seem to act a great deal like the characters they play in this play within a play adapted from a Broadway play. (Got that?) Many memorable songs make this a don't-miss musical, particularly Ann Miller's tap treatment of "Too Darn Hot" and "Why Can't You Behave?" and her remarkable rendering of the great "From This Moment On." It's Miller's movie more than anyone else's, but Grayson and Keel sing the most romantic song in the film, "So in Love," and it really is one of the best songs ever sung on screen. Listen also for the wonderful "Wunderbar," "We Open in Venice," and "Brush Up Your Shakespeare."

## ☐ SMALL TOWN GIRL (1953)

Snazzy song-and-dance routines created by the legendary Busby Berkeley make this film more entertaining than its corny story line might suggest. Small-town life and New York smugness are contrasted in the person of a spoiled rich boy played by Farley Granger and a sweet small-town girl played by Jane Powell, whose lovely soprano is showcased in a church scene ("Lullaby of the Lord") as well as in a jailhouse. Bobby Van dances through the film in top form. His "Jumping Song" through town and "Take Me to Broadway" romp in a closed department store are highlights of the film, second only to Ann Miller's tap routine. Why Jane Powell goes for the snobbish Farley Granger instead of Bobby Van is a mystery! This movie is also like a who's who of film history: Fay Wray (of *King Kong* fame) as the mom, Billie Burke (the good witch in *The Wizard of Oz*) as the snob's mother (you can't miss the voice), the ever-adorable S. Z. Sakall, and a special appearance by the great Nat King Cole.

★BEST *of the* BEST★

## ☐ BRIGADOON (1954)

Spectacular dance sequences against beautiful Scottish backgrounds make this one of the best film adaptations of an Alan Jay Lerner and Frederick Loewe stage play. Gene Kelly and Cyd Charisse—in probably her best screen

role—have never danced more perfectly. Adorable Van Johnson, also in one of his best roles, keeps up with the extraordinary Kelly in every way, especially on "I'll Go Home with Bonnie Jean." This lyrical fantasy, directed by Vincente Minnelli, about a mythical place that comes to life only once every one hundred years, is itself magical, with all its elements perfectly and romantically fused into one seamless tale. "Almost like Being in Love" is the tune that really sticks with you.

Gene Kelly and Cyd Charisse

☐ **CARMEN JONES** (1954) ▦

This movie is a must-see musical on so many levels. French composer Georges Bizet's *Carmen* is here retrofitted with new lyrics by Oscar Hammerstein II, and Hollywood's crème de la crème of African American acting talent make up the cast: Dorothy Dandridge (voiced by Marilyn Horne), singer Harry Belafonte (dubbed by LeVern Hutcherson, whose voice was operatic enough for the part), Pearl Bailey, and Diahann Carroll (also dubbed, despite her lovely singing voice). This is a beautiful film, yet it is difficult to watch because it simply reminds you of the dreadful apartheid society of America before the civil rights movement of the 1960s.

☐ **DEEP IN MY HEART** (1954) ▣

One of the most elaborate biopics of the 1950s, this one, directed by Stanley Donen, traces the life of composer Sigmund Romberg. The treat here is not so much the over-the-top performance of José Ferrer in the starring role, but the specialty numbers with Rosemary Clooney (to whom Ferrer was married, twice), Gene Kelly in a rare dance duet with his brother Fred Kelly, Vic Damone and Jane Powell singing "Will You Remember? (The Sweetheart Song)," Ann Miller and Cyd Charisse at their dancing best, and Tony Martin singing "Lover, Come Back to Me." Helen Traubel is especially noteworthy for her role as Romberg's friend, and her rendition of "Auf Wiedersehn" as Merle Oberon nears death is perhaps the best song in the film.

☐ **THE EDDIE CANTOR STORY** (1954) ▣

Wildly popular in his lifetime, entertainer Eddie Cantor is difficult to understand by today's standards, and Keefe Brasselle's portrayal of Cantor offers little insight into this legendary comedian with the bug eyes. Hearing some of the songs he made famous helps a little, as they are a lot of fun: "If You Knew Susie (Like I Know Susie)," "Ida, Sweet as Apple Cider," "Oh, You Beautiful Doll," and "Makin' Whoopee!"

☐ **THE GLENN MILLER STORY** (1954) ▣

Ten years after his death in an airplane crash over the English Channel during World War II, this biopic about bandleader Glenn Miller features a lot of his arrangements, played by a cast of musicians including drummer Gene Krupa and the legendary Louis Armstrong. James Stewart stars as Miller, with lovable June Allyson as his devoted wife. This film helps you understand

## ☐ SEVEN BRIDES FOR SEVEN BROTHERS (1954) ▦

One of the best of all the 1950s MGM musicals, this film is blessed with a danceable original score by Gene de Paul and Johnny Mercer and the

inspired choreography of Michael Kidd, which move the story along. Enjoying this movie is a guilty pleasure for some people because its take on women makes it politically incorrect these days, even though it is set in Oregon in the mid-nineteenth century. Personally, I always thought the take on men was much more insulting (essentially, they are swine without women). The dance numbers have never been outdone, and what makes them so splendid is the vigor and athleticism of the men and women dancers equally. Howard Keel and Jane Powell star, and they have the voices and vigor to carry the movie.

Nancy Kilgas, Betty Carr, Virginia Gibson, Ruta Kilmonis (aka Ruta Lee), Norma Daggett, and Julie Newmeyer (aka Julie Newmar)

how he developed his unique sound, and through the course of it you get to hear the following songs performed by Glenn Miller's orchestra: "Moonlight Serenade," "Tuxedo Junction," "Little Brown Jug," "St. Louis Blues," "Basin Street Blues," "In the Mood," "A String of Pearls," "Pennsylvania 6-5000," and "American Patrol."

## ☐ LIVING IT UP (1954)

The strange appeal of the comedy team of Dean Martin and Jerry Lewis can perhaps best be understood in this movie, arguably the least off-putting (to scores of people who cannot abide Lewis) of the seventeen films the guys made together. Almost all their films contained music, and Martin was a successful singer in his own right. Here he gets to sing "How Do You Speak to an Angel?" and "Ev'ry Street's a Boulevard in Old New York" (with Lewis), songs that were already known from the Broadway show on which the film is based, *Hazel Flagg.*

### ☐ THERE'S NO BUSINESS LIKE SHOW BUSINESS (1954)

Forget the plot and concentrate on the gorgeous Irving Berlin songs. Marilyn Monroe demonstrates her enduring appeal with "After You Get What You Want, You Don't Want It" and "Heat Wave," and Ethel Merman belts out the title song, making it her own forever, along with "A Pretty Girl Is like a Melody." This is classic showbiz about showbiz.

### ☐ WHITE CHRISTMAS (1954)

One of the hokiest and most dated musicals of all time, this is also one of the most watched. Why? First, there are the songs by Irving Berlin, starting with

---

**★BEST *of the* BEST★**

### ☐ A STAR IS BORN (1954) ▦

Of all the versions of this story, this screenplay by Moss Hart with music by Harold Arlen (who wrote "Over the Rainbow") and lyrics by Ira Gershwin is the best. Under the direction of the legendary George Cukor, Judy Garland has never been more alive on screen. Her rendering of "The Man That Got Away" proved once and for all that her talent went way beyond musical comedy. This is a musical in the sense that the musical numbers are part of the story of Garland's rise to fame, while her actor-husband (played with disturbing realism by James Mason, who never sings a note in the movie) descends into alcoholism and depression. Garland is at her acting best as she sings "Lose That Long Face," trying desperately to pull her husband up and out of the hole he is falling into. I've never forgiven the members of the Academy of Motion Picture Arts and Sciences for passing Judy Garland up for the best actress Oscar in favor of Grace Kelly's vapid performance in *The Country Girl*. Another musical version of *A Star Is Born* appeared in 1976, and I find it almost unwatchable now, despite its stars, Barbra Streisand and Kris Kristofferson, and the movie theme song "Evergreen." It seems to me a good example of Hollywood's inability to create anything authentic out of the sexual revolution and the age of rock and roll.

Judy Garland

the title song, which by 1954 was already a standard, having been introduced a dozen years earlier in *Holiday Inn*. Then there is the great voice of Rosemary Clooney, who, as was the practice in 1950s films, is paired with Bing Crosby, a love interest easily old enough to be her father. None of it really matters; it's all just a trick to get everybody to sing and dance and clown around. Danny Kaye, who can be really cloying on screen, is at his best in this film, all tongue-in-cheek. His mockery of the song "Sisters" with Crosby is hilarious. Dean Jagger's portrayal of the general has probably done as much for Memorial Day as anything this film has done for Christmas.

☐ **DADDY LONG LEGS** (1955)
Ageless dancing legend Fred Astaire is here paired with Leslie Caron, more than thirty years his junior, and the public swallowed it hook, line, and sinker. Mostly it's because everyone knows that musicals of this kind are a setup to display the talents and beauty of their stars, but this one has a substantial story line. Astaire plays a wealthy sponsor who sends Caron, a poor French waif, to college in the United States. Then they fall in love, of course. "Something's Gotta Give" is the standout song in a marvelous score by Johnny Mercer performed by Ray Anthony and His Orchestra. The lovely Mercer ballad "Dream," a popular hit for the Pied Pipers a decade earlier, is revived here. The sets and dance routines are fine examples of what was considered super-modern in the 1950s: big cars, jazz, abstract expressionism, and anything related to Paris.

☐ **I'LL CRY TOMORROW** (1955) ▪
Susan Hayward plays singer and actress Lillian Roth in this biopic, an early raw depiction of alcoholism and abuse that threatened to destroy her life and career.

☐ **IT'S ALWAYS FAIR WEATHER** (1955)
Three World War II buddies vow to reunite after ten years, but when they do, their friendship has fizzled. A day of dealing with romance, boxing, the advertising business, and a newfangled medium called television restores their bond. Gene Kelly, Dan Dailey, and Michael Kidd (the great choreographer) star as the trio, and their dance using trash can lids is a highlight of the film. Cyd Charisse is in great form as she dances with the fighters, and Kelly's astonishing tap dance on roller skates is one of his best ever. The movie is

## ☐ GUYS AND DOLLS (1955)

Who'd have thought that you could make a romantic musical about some gangster lowlifes? Yet, *Guys and Dolls* is exactly that and is often cited as a favorite by film critics. This adaption from Broadway features only one member of the original cast, Vivian Blaine, while casting nonsingers Marlon Brando and Jean Simmons in singing roles, with Frank Sinatra filling out the foursome. As two bet-making gangsters, Sinatra and Brando make a wager over whether or not the latter will be able to seduce Simmons, a sanctimonious missionary setting up shop in their New York City neighborhood. Great songs include "Luck Be a

Marlon Brando, Jean Simmons, Frank Sinatra, and Vivian Blaine

Lady," "I've Never Been in Love Before," "Fugue for Tinhorns (Can Do)," "If I Were a Bell," and "I'll Know," one of the most romantic ditties ever to make its way into a gangster film. The music and lyrics by Frank Loesser provide memorable moments in a score that moves the story along better than the mock tough dialogue. A great reflection of its time, this film is one of the best of many splendid musicals MGM produced.

oddly ahead of its time in the cynicism department, and Dailey's turn as a singing drunk in "Situation Wise" is decidedly unromantic and too dark to be funny.

## ☐ KISMET (1955)

It's fascinating to see Hollywood's version of Baghdad before anyone ever heard of Saddam Hussein (who was eighteen years old in 1955), and where in the world did they find all those whirling dervishes to do their thing behind Howard Keel singing "Fate"? Despite the lavish sets and production quality, this film still seems like a series of music videos (some of which you would not want to see more than once) strung together by a plot involving a poet,

## ☐ OKLAHOMA! (1955)

Filled with immortal songs, this joyous celebration of frontier life in the Oklahoma Territory in the early 1900s brims with American optimism and

youthfulness. The score by Richard Rodgers and Oscar Hammerstein II (the most successful collaboration in the history of musical theater) is brought to life by the beautiful Shirley Jones and handsome Gordon MacRae, with quirky offbeat performances by Charlotte Greenwood, Eddie Albert, Rod Steiger, and Gloria Grahame, whose rendering of "I Cain't Say No" is

Gordon MacRae and Shirley Jones

hilarious. Other memorable songs include "Oh, What a Beautiful Mornin'," "People Will Say We're in Love," "The Surrey with the Fringe on Top," and the sweeping title song. The background of the beautiful American Midwest is central to the adaptation of the play to the screen. Every frame of the film is a great photograph.

his luck, and his daughter. But the songs are among the best ever written for a musical, and some you would want to hear again and again: "Baubles, Bangles, and Beads," "Stranger in Paradise," "And This Is My Beloved," to name just three of the best known. Vic Damone and Ann Blyth sing sweetly but look as if they don't believe themselves to be anywhere but an MGM back lot. Still, this is a Broadway-to-Hollywood fantasy, so laugh and enjoy the music. Keel has a vocal field day begging the wazir not to have his hand chopped off as he sings (what else?) "Gesticulate."

## ☐ LADY AND THE TRAMP (1955)

Blessed with a beautiful score, this Disney animated classic places adorable pooches in the classic male-female dynamic, and the result is pure fun. The spaghetti-eating scene alone is worth its weight in popcorn. Family fare at its finest, and plenty for discussion afterward.

## ☐ LOVE ME OR LEAVE ME (1955)

Everybody knew Doris Day could sing, but this movie proved once and for all that she could act as well. Set in 1920s Chicago and based on the tumultuous life of singer Ruth Etting, the film costars James Cagney in one of the best of his nasty gangster roles. Day reprises "Shakin' the Blues Away."

## ☐ PETE KELLY'S BLUES (1955)

The great Peggy Lee takes on another rare film role, garnering an Oscar nomination for her supporting role in this crime drama with plenty of music starring Jack Webb and Janet Leigh. Among the great songs on the soundtrack are "Somebody Loves Me," "Sing a Rainbow," and "Hard-Hearted Hannah," performed by Ella Fitzgerald.

## ☐ SINCERELY YOURS (1955)

Poor Liberace. Imagine being that talented and that flamboyant at a time when being gay was illegal as well as being classified as a mental illness. Liberace fought allegations of homosexuality until his death from pneumonia related to AIDS in 1987. In 1955, however, he was at the top of his game, arguably the most popular pianist who ever lived. This film offers plenty of insight into his talent and appeal, especially to older women, who saw in him the kind and attentive lover they longed for, made even more sympathetic by the fact that his character copes with losing his hearing by improving the lives of others. The film includes thirty-one piano pieces—everything from Chopin to "The Beer Barrel Polka" and boogie-woogie to *Rhapsody in Blue*. It's almost a time capsule, minus the onstage excesses he ultimately became known (and ridiculed) for. Look for background shots of San Francisco and check out costar Joanne Dru's gorgeous wardrobe. This is the only film in which "Mr. Showmanship" played the lead. At the 1982 Academy Awards ceremony, presenting the award for best original score, Liberace prefaced his performance of selections from each nominee by joking, "I'm very proud of my contribution to motion pictures. I've stopped making them."

## ☐ YOUNG AT HEART (1955)

Doris Day and Frank Sinatra. Teams don't come any better than that, and title songs have never been more infectious and singable than this one. The plot involves three small-town musical sisters, digging clams and roasting marshmallows, who get very competitive where a man (Gig Young) is concerned. Throw in cynical city slicker Frank Sinatra, and the plot thickens—as Doris Day gets more and more adorable. Songwise, it's Sinatra's film, with "Someone to Watch Over Me," "Just One of Those Things," and "One for My Baby (and One More for the Road)" displaying the style that would influence countless imitators for years to come; but Day perfected the art of crying and no one has ever equaled those tears.

☐ **ANYTHING GOES** (1956)
Featuring a host of songs by Cole Porter, Jimmy Van Heusen, and Sammy Cahn, this is another musical about the entertainment business, with Bing Crosby and Donald O'Connor looking for a leading lady and getting wires crossed over Mitzi Gaynor and Zizi Jeanmaire, who dances a dream ballet to "Let's Do It" and "All Through the Night" and performs an over-the-top French-accented "I Get a Kick Out of You." Gaynor and O'Connor sing "It's De-lovely," and the quartet of stars sings "You're the Top." The only problem with the plot and the musical numbers is that they have little or nothing to do with one another, and then there's the matter of Gaynor's singing and Crosby's dancing, and then there's the believability of the romantic entanglements . . . but then, anything goes.

☐ **THE BENNY GOODMAN STORY** (1956) 🖾
Benny Goodman was known as the King of Swing, and his songs "Sing, Sing, Sing," "One O'Clock Jump," "Stompin' at the Savoy," "Moonglow," "Goody Goody," and my favorite "And the Angels Sing" (performed in this film by Martha Tilton) helped define an era. He was still going strong when this movie was made and continued to play his clarinet until his death in 1986 at the age of seventy-seven. While Goodman himself is portrayed as an adult by television pioneer Steve Allen, Goodman's band musicians perform in this film: Gene Krupa, Teddy Wilson, Ben Pollack, Edward "Kid" Ory, and Lionel Hampton. The story makes it clear that Goodman was instrumental in breaking the racial barrier in American music. Gorgeous Donna Reed costars (and blessedly doesn't sing), and Sammy Davis Sr. plays Fletcher Henderson. You'll love the scene where Goodman shows the music snobs that he can play Mozart's Clarinet Concerto with the best of them.

☐ **THE COURT JESTER** (1956) 🎞
Memorable more as a well-written comedy than as a musical, the antics of Danny Kaye, with Angela Lansbury and Glynis Johns, are still amusing today, especially the part in which Kaye starts in with "the vessel with the pestle and the chalice from the palace. . . ."

## ☐ CAROUSEL (1956)

A classic musical, this is a must-see, either on film or on stage, for the songs alone. Most music buffs agree that this show contains some of Rodgers and Hammerstein's sweetest and most enduring work. Shirley Jones and Gordon MacRae are flawless in the roles of Julie Jordan and Billy Bigelow. Today's audiences, however, are liable to giggle at some of the language, especially when Jones is told in song, "You're a Queer One, Julie Jordan." The movie was filmed

Shirley Jones and Barbara Ruick

on location in Maine, and locations such as Boothbay Harbor, Camden, and New Harbor were used, giving the film an authentic feel, despite its rather fantastic premise and dark undertones. The movie was completely passed over at Oscar time. But what a symphony for the ears it is. "The Carousel Waltz" alone is infectious. Add to that "If I Loved You," "June Is Bustin' Out All Over," "What's the Use of Wondrin'," and "You'll Never Walk Alone," and you'll understand what makes this show so unforgettable.

## ☐ THE EDDY DUCHIN STORY (1956)

This life story of the famous pianist and bandleader of the 1930s and 1940s features a slew of great music and songs: "Manhattan," "Brazil," "Ain't She Sweet," Chopin's Nocturne in E-flat Major, op. 9, no. 2, "Exactly like You," "Shine On, Harvest Moon," "Will You Love Me in December as You Do in May?" "Body and Soul," "Dizzy Fingers," "You're My Everything," "On the Sunny Side of the Street," "Let's Fall in Love," and "La vie en rose." Tyrone Power and Kim Novak star, and this is a beautiful film to look at—but no, Power did not do his own piano playing; it was all faked (and rather well) over the playing of the wonderful pianist Carmen Cavallaro.

## ☐ HIGH SOCIETY (1956)

This is a musical remake of *The Philadelphia Story*, made apparently to showcase a selection of tunes by Cole Porter—and to provide a vehicle for stars Bing Crosby and Frank Sinatra to sing their duet "Well, Did You Evah?" Among the tunes that linger after the final act is the beautiful theme song, "True Love." And yes, the stunning Grace Kelly does sing in this film, although you won't remember much of it. This is what was known in the 1950s as "smart and sophisticated," but I tend to see it as stuffy. It is also part of the trend in the 1950s to pair big stars like Crosby with love interests half their age. Couldn't they have sung to their daughters once in a while?

★ BEST *of the* BEST ★

## ☐ THE KING AND I (1956)

Set in the late 1860s, this musical about culture clash is remarkable for its deft adaptation of a stage play to the screen through the use of gorgeous sets that seem exotic yet still allowed American audiences to relate to a remote

Deborah Kerr and Yul Brynner

Southeast Asian culture, however Hollywoodish its rendering. There is hardly a song or a musical number that is not memorable. Then there is the casting: Yul Brynner, although of Russian descent, seems to have been born to play the King of Siam, and Deborah Kerr, although her voice was dubbed by the glorious Marni Nixon, Hollywood's greatest dubber, dances like a dream and defined British elegance for generations of American moviegoers. Memorable songs include "Whistle a Happy Tune," "Hello Young Lovers," "Getting to Know You," and the delightful "March of the Siamese Children." The topper, however is Brynner and Kerr dancing the polka to "Shall We Dance?" Although the child performers in this film are endearing, it is a movie for adults, and the music by Richard Rodgers and Oscar Hammerstein II is some of their most sophisticated work. Warner Bros. produced an animated version of the show in 1999.

## ☐ INVITATION TO THE DANCE (1956)

It might better have been called *Invitation to the Pantomime*, because there is no speaking, much less singing, in the film, a production much better suited to the stage. The movie does in fact look like a filmed stage production, and the format and ambitions of the film are not what audiences had come to expect from Gene Kelly. But this was his baby, and he wanted to take filmed dance to entirely new levels of artistic achievement. In many ways, it is a testimony to his power as a choreographer and a star that he was able to pull it off. Nevertheless, beautiful as it is, this is not everyone's cup of tea. Watching the first of the three dance sequences, I longed for Kelly to take that white paint off his mime face and stop mooning over the ballerina. He did, and the next two sequences are more enjoyable, the last being rather fun when animation takes over.

## ☐ FUNNY FACE (1957)

What a pleasure it is to see Audrey Hepburn romp through this film with style *and* her own voice. A witty spoof of the fashion industry, with Broadway legend Kay Thompson hamming it up as a magazine executive singing "Think Pink" as she plans a marketing promotion. "I wouldn't attempt to tell a woman what a woman ought to think, but tell her if she's gotta think, think pink!" Alive with the fashions of the 1950s, the film pairs Hepburn with Fred Astaire, thirty years her senior, and you can almost buy it, especially when they dance, largely because of Astaire's charming screen presence. Other numbers to look for: Hepburn, after the fashion magazine staff invades her bookstore, singing "How Long Has This Been Going On?"; Astaire singing the title song in his photographer's darkroom; and the upbeat, romantic, and undeniably charming "Bonjour Paris," as the bookstore clerk begins transforming into a fashion model. Music and lyrics are by the unbeatable George and Ira Gershwin, culminating with "'s Wonderful." Main drawbacks: the movie spends an inordinate amount of time satirizing the existentialist philosophers and artists of the day and fusses excessively over the deep meaning of Astaire's true love for this young girl.

## ☐ THE HELEN MORGAN STORY (1957) ▐

You may remember Helen Morgan from the 1936 version of *Show Boat*. This film biography, starring Ann Blyth and Paul Newman, shows her rise from sordid beginnings to fame and fortune through her decline and death

## ☐ THE PAJAMA GAME (1957)

One of the finest of all of Doris Day's fine musicals, *The Pajama Game* is filled with memorable songs, including "I'm Not at All in Love," "Hey There," "Hernando's Hideaway," and "There Once Was a Man (I Love You More)." Carol Haney dancing to "Steam Heat" is a real treat, and "I'll Never Be Jealous Again a(Picture This)," the duet between Reta Shaw and Eddie Foy Jr. is thoroughly enjoyable and once again features an old pair joyously singing and dancing. John Raitt (singer Bonnie Raitt's father) has a beautiful voice, and Doris Day radiates like a small sun bouncing across the screen. It's romantic fun and a great example of Bob Fosse's inventive choreography. It is also interesting to note that the central conflict in the film is at the pajama factory between management (Raitt) and the union (Day), and she consistently refuses to accept his patronizing promises as he woos her.

due to alcoholism. Gogi Grant did the singing for Blyth, once again leaving average viewers bewildered by the decision to cast someone who cannot sing as a singer. This film features many great songs that Morgan made famous during her lifetime, among them "Can't Help Lovin' Dat Man" and "Bill" from *Show Boat*, "Why Was I Born?" "Ain't She Sweet," "Baby Face," "If You Were the Only Girl in the World," "Avalon," "The One I Love Belongs to Somebody Else," "Love Nest," "Do, Do, Do," "Breezin' Along with the Breeze," "The Man I Love," "On the Sunny Side of the Street," "Someone to Watch Over Me," "Deep Night," "April in Paris," and "You Do Something to Me."

## ☐ JAILHOUSE ROCK (1957) 🎬

Even if you cannot bear to watch this movie all the way through, you must see Elvis "the Pelvis" Presley gyrate his hips through the title song.

## ☐ THE JOKER IS WILD (1957)

Frank Sinatra plays a comedian and singer in trouble with the mob in this biopic based on the life of Joe E. Lewis. Sinatra gets to sing the wonderful "All the Way."

## ☐ LES GIRLS (1957)

This was Gene Kelly's last musical for MGM studios. He partnered with a trio of leading ladies—Mitzi Gaynor, Kay Kendall, Taina Elg—and fittingly ended his contract with a Cole Porter film score (also his last), as he had begun it, and in Paris, which he loved—although the tunes tend to be some of his less familiar,

---

★ BEST *of the* BEST ★

## ☐ DAMN YANKEES (1958)

One of the main reasons to watch this fantasy film is that it is a successful adaption from stage to screen that presents clever songs that give more insight into life in the 1950s than *The Catcher in the Rye*. Innuendo is everywhere. Look at Gwen Verdon, the Broadway sensation and wife and protégé of Bob Fosse (who brought to life so many Broadway tunes and did the chore-

Albert Linville, Nat Frey, Russ Brown, and Jimmie Komack

ography for this film). Listen to handsome Tab Hunter, charming and the perfect 1958 man. "Whatever Lola Wants" is a great tune, made even more amusing than its lyrics by the over-the-top rendition by Verdon, who was only six years older than Hunter but looks like she could be his mother. There are songs here that keep forever, such as "(You Gotta Have) Heart." If you remember *All in the Family*, you'll love seeing Jean Stapleton's role in this film, and *My Favorite Martian* fans will love Ray Walston in "Those Were the Good Old Days." "Goodbye, Old Girl" has to be one of the sweetest songs ever written. Take note of Rae Allen as she sings "Shoeless Joe from Hannibal Mo." and blows away the trope of women reporters in the locker room years and years before it became an issue. And dancing baseball players—how much fun is that? Notice they are not all white; you can see change a comin' to America. Fosse himself and Verdon do a sensational duet in "Who's Got the Pain?"

including the title song, "Ça c'est l'amour," "Ladies in Waiting," "You're Just Too, Too!" "Why Am I So Gone about That Gal?" "The Rope Song," and "Be a Clown" (which he sang with Judy Garland in *The Pirate*). The story line is complicated by the fact that it's told over and over again from all the major players' points of view. Kelly is just old enough and accomplished enough for his womanizing to seem less than charming and his modernist dance numbers less than great. Still, it's pretty to look at, and it's Gene Kelly after all *avec les* beautiful girls.

## ☐ PAL JOEY (1957)

Frank Sinatra stars as charming Joey Evans, a womanizer who loves 'em and leaves 'em—handsome, funny, talented, and a first-class, A-number-one heel. When Joey meets the former chorus girl and now rich widow played by Rita Hayworth, it appears to be a match made in heaven—until Joey is smitten by a sexier and younger chorus girl played by Kim Novak. During the course of this messing around, an astonishing number of marvelous songs get sung, including "Bewitched, Bothered, and Bewildered," "I Could Write a Book," "I Didn't Know What Time It Was," "The Lady Is a Tramp," and "My Funny Valentine." I never realized just how good a singer Frank Sinatra was until I saw this movie.

★ BEST *of the* BEST ★

## ☐ GIGI (1958) ▦

Maurice Chevalier's lecherous rendition of "Thank Heaven for Little Girls" notwithstanding, this is one of the most delightful of all the MGM musicals. With a score by Alan Jay Lerner and Frederick Loewe, and under the direction

of Vincente Minnelli, the film is witty and replete with every cliché about the wonders of Paris—made all the more delightful by the total Frenchness of Leslie Caron in the title role. At twenty-seven, she plays Gigi as she blossoms from giddy teenager to sophisticated adult. "The Night They Invented Champagne" is an exuberant highlight, while Chevalier is quite bearable in a clever duet with Hermione Gingold titled "I Remember It Well."

Leslie Caron

## ☐ SILK STOCKINGS (1957)

This musical version of the Greta Garbo film *Ninotchka* stars Fred Astaire, Cyd Charisse, and Janis Paige (as a mock Esther Williams swimming star). When it comes to musical plots, less can be more, and in this case there is a

## ☐ SOUTH PACIFIC (1958)

Mitzi Gaynor

*South Pacific* is full of beautiful, memorable songs, and they move the story along and reveal the inner feelings of the characters. Based on a successful Broadway show by Richard Rodgers and Oscar Hammerstein II, the film makes the best of cinema's ability to convey a sense of place. Rosanno Brazzi and Mitzi Gaynor star, but according to the Internet Movie Database, there are probably more dubbed singing voices in this film than in any other screen version of a Rodgers and Hammerstein musical, although the only dubber who receives screen credit is Giorgio Tozzi, who dubs for Brazzi. This is because Tozzi was a renowned bass-baritone with the Metropolitan Opera. The film tackles the issue of racism and seems to want us to understand the root of it by making Brazzi's relationship with a native girl central to the plot and contrasting it with an American soldier in love with an island girl. The film was remade for TV in 2001 with Glenn Close, and it took the racism theme further, which only made concentrating on the music that much more difficult. In either version, there has never been a better set of songs than "There Is Nothing like a Dame," "Bali Ha'i," "A Cockeyed Optimist," "Some Enchanted Evening," "I'm Gonna Wash That Man Right Outta My Hair," "This Nearly Was Mine," "Happy Talk," and my personal favorite, "Younger Than Springtime." Imagine the power of these lyrics when the show opened on Broadway in 1949: "You've got to be taught to hate and fear, you've got to be taught from year to year. It's got to be drummed in your dear little ear. You've got to be carefully taught. You've got to be taught to be afraid of people whose eyes are oddly made, and people whose skin is a different shade. You've got to be carefully taught."

## ☐ PORGY AND BESS (1959) 🎞

There has never been a set of songs more poignant or heartbreaking than "Summertime," "It Ain't Necessarily So," "I Loves You Porgy," and "Bess, You Is My Woman Now." It just doesn't get any better. Although written by white composer George Gershwin as a "folk opera" that debuted in 1935, this film adaptation rang absolutely true in the racially segregated era that preceded the American civil rights movement of the 1960s. Could Porgy without the use

Sidney Poitier and Dorothy Dandridge

of his legs be any more symbolic of the way America emasculated African American men? What this movie achieved is made even more awesome by the reality of race relations in the United States before the civil rights movement. Some of the greatest talents of the era came together to bring this Broadway play to the screen: Dorothy Dandridge, Sidney Poitier, Sammy Davis Jr., Pearl Bailey, and a very young Diahann Carroll, all of whom later went on to break one racial barrier after another. Set in a 1912 fishing village in South Carolina, this opera lacks the glamour of a lot of Hollywood productions, but not the soul. Other versions of *Porgy and Bess* have been staged and filmed, but this movie gives you a sense of what black people in the United States have been up against since the founding of this nation, and it makes something beautiful out of something ugly. Robert McFerrin dubbed the singing voice for Poitier's Porgy, and Adele Addison sang for Dandridge as Bess. Ruth Attaway's Serena and Diahann Carroll's Clara were also dubbed. Although Dandridge and Carroll were singers, their voices were not considered operatic enough. Sammy Davis Jr., Brock Peters, and Pearl Bailey (who played Sportin' Life, Crown, and Maria, respectively) were the only principals who provided their own singing. André Previn's adaptation of the score won him an Academy Award, the film's only Oscar. The film was removed from release in 1974 by the Gershwin estate and can now only be seen in film archives or on bootleg videos. Check with your library. It's obvious as you watch this film that it was a meagerly financed production compared to other musicals of this caliber, but the talent, the heart, the genius of the music triumph.

lot of Soviet agent stuff to ignore. It's the Cole Porter songs that matter. It's fun to watch Charisse play a super-serious Soviet while Astaire makes jokes about the whole spy act, but the real highlight of the film may well be watching Charisse put on her underwear.

### ☐ LI'L ABNER (1959)

What a hokey little creation this is, the ultimate hillbilly satire. But wait, listen to the political commentary. Timeless. I remember hearing about this movie when I was a twelve-year-old in Michigan. Something of a fuss was being made because Al Capp's popular comic strip was coming to the screen and everybody was going to be able to see Li'l Abner, Daisy Mae, Mammy and Pappy Yokum, and the rest of the inhabitants of Dogpatch as real people, all fussing over Sadie Hawkins Day. I knew older kids in our school went to Sadie Hawkins dances so the girls could chase after the boys. Fast-forward to 2012 and I'm trying to track this movie down. Never saw it, and it's hard to find, so I end up downloading it as a digital file from Amazon.com and watching it on my computer. You gotta see it. Granted, it looks like a filmed stage play, and the songs and jokes are fabulously dated, but Michael Kidd's choreography has captured this Broadway show for posterity. Look at the cast list for familiar names from before they were famous. Peter Palmer and Leslie Parrish in the lead roles are impossibly gorgeous, and then Julie Newmar somehow outshines them.

### ☐ SOME LIKE IT HOT (1959) 🎞

Although this is more a comedy than a musical, there is plenty about the film that makes it essential to any study of musicals. Jack Lemmon and Tony Curtis play musicians, first of all, who are being pursued by gangsters because they have witnessed a murder. Masquerading as women, they go on tour with an all-girl band. Marilyn Monroe sings "Running Wild" on a train to Florida, and the rest is movie history.

Tony Curtis, Marilyn Monroe, and Jack Lemmon star in *Some Like It Hot*.

# SOCIAL CHANGE

Values, Virtues, and Validation

ENERALLY THOUGHT OF AS A DECADE OF REBELLION and protest, the 1960s in the world of movie musicals actually enjoyed a good deal of spillover from the golden age, giving us *West Side Story, The Music Man, My Fair Lady, The Sound of Music, Oliver!,* and *Hello, Dolly!* (and the annoying practice of punctuating Broadway show titles with an exclamation point, *Tiresome!*). By 1969, however, the American taste for Rodgers and Hammerstein and Lerner and Loewe had peaked; a more cynical era was about to begin.

One of the centerpieces of this decade is the peerless French classic *The Umbrellas of Cherbourg.* An unlikely candidate for immortality in America, this film has nevertheless captured the hearts of many an American musical lover, including me. Completely free of spoken dialogue and sung entirely in French, this touching tale of star-crossed lovers is unique in film history, a gorgeous film, much like an opera, where the subtitles are barely needed for you to follow the plot.

The decade also gave children what has become a beloved classic, *Mary Poppins.* But as you watch the musicals of the 1960s, you can feel the end coming in the struggle to make everything come up roses in *Gypsy*, the half-hearted adoration of Paris in *Can-Can*, Doris Day singing her heart out in *Jumbo*, Fred Astaire giving it his all in *Finian's Rainbow*, and Debbie Reynolds bellying up to the bar in *The Unsinkable Molly Brown*. You then know that the ship of romantic musicals is going down as sure as the *Titanic*.

☐ **BELLS ARE RINGING** (1960)

The question to ask when you are watching this musical is how well the humor holds up, since more time is spent on getting laughs than singing songs. Judy Holliday's vulnerable/meddling character and Dean Martin's debonair/immature counterpart seem to be an unlikely romantic combination. In this translation of a long-running Broadway show to film, Holliday stars as a Brooklyn telephone answering service operator who falls for a client. This gets complicated—and contrived—but creates many opportunities for Holliday and Martin to sing great songs by Jule Styne, with lyrics by the incomparable Betty Comden and Adolph Green, including the classics "Just in Time" and "The Party's Over." Production numbers like the one in which Eddie Foy Jr. explains how an undercover racetrack betting system will work, "It's a Simple Little System," actually are more watchable than the ongoing intrigue over the lead characters' love lives. This film does not adequately convey Judy Holliday's enormous appeal as a stage performer, but, if nothing else, it is a marvelous record of what telephones meant in people's lives before they were mobile.

☐ **CAN-CAN** (1960)

Set in 1890s Paris, the Broadway show on which the film is based was a huge success, with its fabulous and naughty cancan dance, re-created here by Juliet Prowse, the most watchable performer in the entire film. The music of Cole Porter—"You Do Something to Me," "C'est magnifique," "It's All Right with Me," "Let's Do It," and "I Love Paris"—is worth all the waiting through silly debates over the immorality of the cancan. Frank Sinatra is his usual sophisticated self, although it's hard to buy him as French. In fact, the biggest mistake in the film is having Frenchmen Maurice Chevalier (whose charms have always been lost on me) and Louis Jourdan around to make us believe we are in Paris; Prowse fakes a French accent reasonably well, but Sinatra and Shirley MacLaine twanging away in American English makes the contrast quite grating on the ears.

## ☐ **PEPE** (1960)

For a film that was nominated for seven Academy Awards, this odd little movie is pretty hard to find a half century after it was made. Starring Mario Moreno (aka Cantinflas), already hugely popular in his native Mexico, it served as another showcase for a bevy of American singers. The plot premise casts Cantinflas as Pepe, a ranch hand who goes to Hollywood to retrieve a horse. There he meets one movie star after another. Shirley Jones costars and sings the title song, and there are cameo appearances by Maurice Chevalier, Bing Crosby, Bobby Darin, Sammy Davis Jr., Jimmy Durante, Zsa Zsa Gabor, Greer Garson, Frank Sinatra . . . see how many you can spot! The problem is the condescension with which Cantinflas is treated, while at the same time he seems to be trying way too hard to be liked by American audiences. Ignore all that and enjoy the location shots and the great music. When I saw the movie at the age of thirteen, my favorite moment was hearing Judy Garland sing "Faraway Part of Town," although I was sorely disappointed—having convinced my poor mother to drive eighteen miles to the nearest drive-in theater—that she never appears on screen.

☐ **BABES IN TOYLAND** (1961)

There are two reasons to watch this rather silly piece of fluff. One is to get some sense of why Annette Funicello, a former Disney Mousketeer, was so popular; the other is to see the venerable Ray Bolger (the scarecrow in *The Wizard of Oz*) still going strong as he dances to "Castle in Spain."

☐ **BLUE HAWAII** (1961)

Happy to be out of the army and back home in Hawaii with his surfboard and his beach buddies, Elvis Presley—playing as in all his films a version of Elvis Presley—hits new levels of wholesomeness as he sings "I Can't Help Falling in Love." The film is hilarious for its depiction of the mores of the day, before the sexual revolution. The Hawaiian visitors bureau owes a big debt to Elvis for popularizing the state as a tourist destination; Hawaii became a state just two years before the film's release. And watch for Angela Lansbury's turn as his snobbish Southern belle mother. "Ito Eats" is Presley's blatant Harry Belafonte imitation.

☐ **FLOWER DRUM SONG** (1961) ▦

Although the Broadway show did not produce many hit songs, watching this film version of the popular musical comedy offers an opportunity to appreciate just how wonderful many of the songs are, in particular the deceptively simple "A Hundred Million Miracles." Not surprising, since the music is by the incomparable team of Richard Rodgers and Oscar Hammerstein II. "I Enjoy Being a Girl," sung by gorgeous Nancy Kwan, has been recorded by many singers and even parodied in a Gap commercial by Sarah Jessica Parker. "Grant Avenue" belongs in the pantheon of great songs about San Francisco, and "You Are Beautiful" echoes the simple wisdom of "A Hundred Million Miracles." Of course, this musical is a popularized version of what it means to be Chinese in America, but the show deals seriously with the controversial issue of illegal immigration. "Where are you from?" a police officer asks Miyoshi Umeki and her father, who have sneaked into the United States as cargo from China. "The East," they respond. "Oh, New York?" says the officer. "No, further east," the father quips. Umeki is disarmingly amusing in her assessments of American culture, although some critics in the Chinese community objected to her being given the role, since she was of Japanese descent.

## ☐ WEST SIDE STORY (1961)

If you've already seen this 1961 American musical classic, you might not remember that the central conflict in the movie is between the Puerto Ricans and the "Polacks" in New York. Played by Richard Beymer, Tony is the good-hearted Polish boy who falls in love with Maria, the good-hearted Puerto Rican girl played by Natalie Wood, setting off a gang war. Wood's voice is dubbed, once again by the great Marni Nixon, but she is otherwise perfect as Maria, singing "I Feel Pretty." The more times I see this movie, however, the more I think it belongs to Rita Moreno, who sings the classics "America" and "A Boy like That" with such passion that it is more relevant today than ever, applied to any ethnic group struggling to succeed in the land of  liberty. Although true to the 1950s setting, much of the lingo and behavior was already considered corny when the movie came out, but a musical about ethnic warfare, in which gangs leap about and sing, revolutionized musical theater and cinema in countless ways. The music by Leonard Bernstein and lyrics by Stephen Sondheim are as lovely today as the day they were written, especially "Maria" and "Tonight."

## ☐ GYPSY (1962)

Two great songs stand out in this musical biography, loosely based on the life of stripper Gypsy Rose Lee: "Let Me Entertain You" (very easy to strip to) and "Everything's Coming Up Roses." While you may think the life story of a stripper is too naughty a topic for family night at the movies, I can assure you there is nothing particularly raunchy in this film. In fact, Natalie Wood in the title role never completely disrobes; she teases and titillates instead. This is really a movie about vaudeville and the days when men were men and strippers left something to the imagination. The dynamic and talented Rosalind Russell does a respectable job as Mama Rose, but she is no singing match for Ethel Merman, who originated the role on Broadway but lost out on the film part.

### ☐ JUMBO (1962)
Also known as *Billy Rose's Jumbo*, this film marked the end of Busby Berkeley's career, and it was not particularly well received by audiences or critics. But there are many reasons to watch this beautifully filmed circus epic, Doris Day and Jimmy Durante among them. As someone who has never been a fan of circuses or clowns or dancing elephants, I still enjoy watching all the talent

★ BEST *of the* BEST ★

### ☐ THE MUSIC MAN (1962) 🎞
Remarkable for its originality, Meredith Wilson's *The Music Man* has never been equaled for unabashed Americana. Every song is a comedic paean to a way of life now lost to history. The film pokes fun at many sacred cows and exposes the hypocrisy small-town respectability often masks. The opening song is as close to rap as anyone ever got in 1962, and the quaint, old-fashioned settings are happily and lovingly mocked with every tune. It has always seemed ironic to me that librarians often disliked "Marian the Librarian" because the character was a stereotype of the shushing librarian. Although Shirley Jones does indeed do a bit of shushing in the role, she is also the most beautiful and intelligent woman in town, and the only citizen with enough street smarts to immediately see Professor Harold Hill, as played by Robert Preston, for the fake he is. Among the loveliest songs in the film are "Goodnight, My Someone" and "Till There Was You."

Shirley Jones and Robert Preston

on parade in this movie. Real circus performers contribute to the authentic feel of the film, and its musical sections are top-notch, especially Day singing "This Can't Be Love" (while riding a white horse), "My Romance," and "Little Girl Blue," as well as her duet with Martha Raye on "Why Can't I?"

## ☐ THE WONDERFUL WORLD OF THE BROTHERS GRIMM (1962)

This seldom-watched little gem is a must for fans of television's *Once upon a Time* or *Grimm*. Notable for its "Dancing Princess" number featuring Russ Tamblyn and Yvette Mimieux, the film is a fictionalized, partly musical biography of Jacob and Wilhelm Grimm, the great nineteenth-century collectors of folktales, bringing to life three of their stories, "The Dancing Princess," "The Cobbler and the Elves," and "The Singing Bone." Laurence Harvey and Claire Bloom star, and it's also fun to watch for appearances by such television personalities as Barbara Eden, Jim Backus, and Arnold Stang.

## ☐ BYE BYE BIRDIE (1963)

Realizing after the film was completed that Ann-Margret was the hottest commodity in cinema, the studio slapped on an extra number of her screeching the title song and tried to bill her as the real star. Actually, "How Lovely to Be a Woman" and "A Lot of Livin' to Do" are quite sufficient to show what a talent she was. Meanwhile, the real love story, starring Janet Leigh and Dick Van Dyke, gets buried. Adapted from the play of the same name, the film features several cute comedy bits about being a teenager, and some great romantic tunes, the best of which is "Put On a Happy Face." "The Telephone Hour" and Paul Lynde's rendering of "Kids" are very funny. If you like *Grease*, remember, this one came first. Television icon Ed Sullivan plays himself in a central role in the film; he can't act or sing, but he provides the setup that had everybody in the movie theater thinking of Elvis Presley's well-publicized induction into the army.

## ☐ A HARD DAY'S NIGHT (1964)

Even when it was released in 1964, this black-and-white oddity was not what anybody expected from the sensational Beatles. As a result, it is much more interesting years later than anyone could have expected. Instead of adding to the Beatles mythology, it brings the boys down to earth in quirky and eccentric ways, presenting some great songs in the process. Early Beatles was all about silliness, and this is a fine example of that, although it may leave you

### ☐ MY FAIR LADY (1964)

I've long thought that everything about this film adaptation of the highly successful Broadway play is perfect—except the decision to use a voice double (Marni Nixon, yet again) for Audrey Hepburn. Julie Andrews

fans have taken a long time to forgive the powers that be for choosing Hepburn for the part over Andrews, who originated the role. It's time to admit that Hepburn turns in the performance of a lifetime, cockney accent and all, as Eliza Doolittle in this musical interpretation of the George Bernard Shaw play *Pygmalion.* The story in a nutshell: A misogynistic and snobbish phonetics professor agrees to a wager that he can take a poor flower girl and make her presentable in high society. Listen to

Audrey Hepburn and Jeremy Brett

the way "Wouldn't It Be Loverly?" is spoken and sung seamlessly. There's never been a more romantic song than "I Could Have Danced All Night," unless it's "On the Street Where You Live." "Get Me to the Church on Time," "With a Little Bit of Luck," and "The Rain in Spain" glisten with wit and tension. "I've Grown Accustomed to Her Face" is the pivotal moment when you know that Eliza Doolittle has won over the arrogant Professor Higgins.

wondering what all the fuss was about. It takes forever to get to the songs, so this ends up less a musical and more a study, or a long and somewhat tedious music video.

### ☐ MARY POPPINS (1964)

This Disney film looks deceptively simple, but it has lived in the hearts of children for more than half a century, and continues to charm new generations. After losing out on the role of Eliza Doolittle in *My Fair Lady*, a role she created on Broadway, Julie Andrews was swept to superstardom and an

Oscar with this tale of an uncanny nanny. Dick Van Dyke does a remarkable job as a cockney chimney sweep, and his comic and dancing skills are on full display, especially in "Chim Chim Cheree." Andrews is unforgettable singing "A Spoonful of Sugar" and "Supercalifragilisticexpialidocious." Set in England in 1910, the changing times for women are captured not only by Andrews's assertive nanny but by the delightful Glynis Johns singing the hilarious "Sister Suffragette."

### ☐ ROBIN AND THE 7 HOODS (1964)

Frank Sinatra introduces the world to "My Kind of Town, Chicago," in this testosterone-infused Prohibition-era gangster spoof, also starring Dean Martin, Bing Crosby, Sammy Davis Jr., and Peter Falk.

★BEST *of the* BEST★

### ☐ THE UMBRELLAS OF CHERBOURG (1964)

Michel Legrand's classic of French cinema is more like an opera than a typical musical. The film's dialogue is all sung as recitative, even the most casual conversation. The beautiful melody "I Will Wait for You" reappears seamlessly and ironically throughout the film. Directed by Jacques Demy and starring Catherine Deneuve and Nino Castelnuovo, the movie tells the story of star-crossed young lovers who are separated after she becomes pregnant. It seems they must be headed for a happy ending, but there is more to the tale than that. The snowy scene at the end is a real tearjerker. Every stylish frame of the film is like a work of modern art. *Umbrellas* is the middle film in an informal "romantic trilogy" of Demy films that share some of the same

Catherine Deneuve and Anne Vernon

actors, characters, and overall look; it comes after *Lola* (1961) and before *The Young Girls of Rochefort* with Gene Kelly (1968), both interesting to watch for many of the same reasons. Translation alert: You do not need subtitles to understand what is happening in the film.

## ☐ RUDOLPH THE RED-NOSED REINDEER (1964) 🎬

Although not technically on the silver screen, this animated television special is worth including here. Sam the snowman, with the familiar voice of singer Burl Ives, narrates the tale of Rudolph, a story written as a Montgomery Ward marketing tool in 1939 and turned into a popular song by Gene Autry ten years later. The story, the song, and the film continue to delight young and old alike, year after year, and this is certainly a must-see around the Christmas holiday.

## ☐ THE UNSINKABLE MOLLY BROWN (1964) 🎬

My favorite parts of this movie come when Debbie Reynolds sings "I Ain't Down Yet" and "Belly Up to the Bar, Boys." Her performance as Molly Brown earned her an Oscar nomination, and I have to say she gives this film her all. The rags-to-riches tale is based on the life of a woman who actually survived the sinking of the *Titanic*. Music and lyrics are by Meredith Wilson, who also gave us *The Music Man*. "I'm gonna learn to read and write," says Molly before she leaves her mountain cabin in search of a rich husband and a better life. She's every librarian's dream.

## ☐ VIVA LAS VEGAS (1964)

Elvis Presley and Ann-Margret go on a tear through Las Vegas during its first Grand Prix, leaving the title song etched in the collective brain of America. It's not hard to imagine as you watch this film why "Elvis impersonator" became a bona fide profession after the singer's death. Elvis is pretty much impersonating himself in this movie, except when he is impersonating Ray Charles on the great song "What'd I Say?"

## ☐ BEACH BLANKET BINGO (1965)

A slice of the '60s before they got serious, this is arguably the best of a slew of "Beach" movies that feature romantic songs and lots of cavorting along the seashore in California. You'll love watching these perfect teenagers, led by Annette Funicello and Frankie Avalon, as they shake their stuff to the title tune. The movie costars a lip-synching Linda Evans (later of TV's *The Big Valley* and *Dynasty*) as Sugar Kane and features comedy by Paul Lynde, Don Rickles, and the legendary Buster Keaton.

☐ **HELP!** (1965)

The sole purpose of this movie is to showcase a bunch of songs by the Beatles. The plot has the four mop heads chasing around trying to protect Ringo from a cult. This is the second film in which Ringo Starr, George Harrison, Paul

---

★BEST *of the* BEST★

☐ **THE SOUND OF MUSIC** (1965) 🎞️

When the film came out in 1965, six years after the show opened on Broadway, countless classes from schools across the country made this their senior trip or class outing for the year. So it was with my class at Armada High School in Michigan. We had to see it on the big screen, and when Julie Andrews twirled into view singing the title song it changed our lives. I don't think anybody could have predicted that nearly fifty years later we'd still be humming tunes from this marvelous score by Richard Rodgers and Oscar Hammerstein II. From the opening song to the improbable escape from the Nazis with the assistance of the nuns from the abbey, we are enthralled, viewing after viewing, and I can say with certainty that it has everything to do with the songs. "My Favorite Things," for example, has withstood numerous interpretations,

Julie Andrews

including saxophonist John Coltrane's classic jazz rendition. Yes, the children are cute, Christopher Plummer handsome, and Julie Andrews enchanting, but it is the songs that make this show: "Climb Every Mountain," "The Lonely Goatherd," "Sixteen Going on Seventeen," "Something Good," "Do Re Mi," "So Long, Farewell," and "Edelweiss" are all memorable and make you want to listen to them again and again. See if you can spot dubber extraordinaire Marni Nixon as one of the singing nuns.

McCartney, and John Lennon basically play themselves (the first was *A Hard Day's Night*), and it is essential. You get to hear the classics "You're Gonna Lose That Girl," "You've Got to Hide Your Love Away," "Ticket to Ride," "I'm Happy Just to Dance with You," and many others.

☐ **A FUNNY THING HAPPENED ON THE WAY TO THE FORUM** (1966)
Another translation from stage to film, this production benefits from lavish sets and the kind of scenery that only film can offer. The satirizing of life in ancient Rome is overlaid with the mentality of the 1960s, so the eunuch jokes, the slave and virgin jokes, and the titillating girlie dances seem like soft-core porn, and they have no relation to Rome except as it serves as a design motif. Musically the movie offers a catchy theme song, "Comedy Tonight," some clever puns, and the rather hummable "Lovely." My guess is that children would be bored silly by this movie. I was, and the charms of Zero Mostel, Jack Gilford, and Phil Silvers are still completely lost on me.

☐ **THE SINGING NUN** (1966)
Hot on the heels of the real French musical sensation Soeur Sourire, hyped internationally as the Singing Nun, comes this Hollywood version of her life story, with none other than Debbie Reynolds in the lead role. After you watch this, check out the real Singing Nun on YouTube.

☐ **CAMELOT** (1967)
The beautiful music of Alan Jay Lerner and Frederick Loewe is reason enough to watch this 179-minute epic adapted from the wildly successful stage play of the same name. Although Julie Andrews introduced these songs on Broadway, she was once again (as with *My Fair Lady*) passed over for the lead in favor of Vanessa Redgrave, who does a decent singing job and looks ravishing as Guinevere to Richard Harris's King Arthur. Harris speak-sings his songs, but Franco Nero sings admirably as the smoldering, arrogant Sir Lancelot. It's a lovely romantic film, most notably in the song "If Ever I Would Leave You," sung to Guinevere by Lancelot as their illicit love affair is on the verge of exposure.

☐ **DOCTOR DOLITTLE** (1967)
Rex Harrison (*My Fair Lady*) stars in this fantasy about a man who communicates with animals exceptionally well. Harrison talk-sings the movie's most famous tune, "Talk to the Animals." Costar Samantha Eggar's vocals are

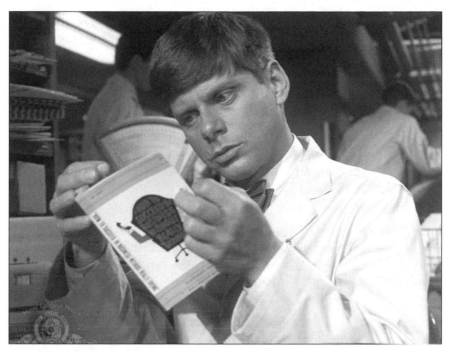

Robert Morse in *How to Succeed in Business without Really Trying*

provided by Diana Lee. This is still good family fare, and it was remade in 1998 with Eddie Murphy in the starring role and lots of pop music thrown in for good measure.

☐ **HOW TO SUCCEED IN BUSINESS WITHOUT REALLY TRYING** (1967)
"I Believe in You" is a real showstopper, and this film version of the Broadway smash of the same name makes good use of the song—and the rest of the score by Frank Loesser. Robert Morse stars as a schemer who's scamming his way to the top of the executive heap. The movie lampoons corporate America, but in a way that actually celebrates it at the same time. The underrated Michele Lee does a splendid job as the love interest, and it's marvelous to see old matinee idol and musical star Rudy Vallee pulled out of mothballs, singing and having a field day with Morse in their roles as musical *Mad Men*. (Perhaps you will recognize Morse as Bert Cooper on the hot AMC series?)

☐ **THE JUNGLE BOOK** (1967) 🌞
A marvelous Disney animated feature inspired by Rudyard Kipling's nineteenth-century story collection, this is the tale of a boy who has been

raised by wolves in the jungles of India. On a long journey to be reunited with other humans, the boy meets many animal characters in this exciting musical that might attract boys reluctant to watch musicals.

☐ **THOROUGHLY MODERN MILLIE** (1967)

Julie Andrews and Mary Tyler Moore sing and quip their way through this movie comedy scored by Elmer Bernstein and André Previn. The word "zany" best describes this spoof of the Roaring Twenties, with Andrews as an innocent country girl who comes to the big city in search of a husband. Veteran performer Carol Channing as a rich and nutty "jazz baby" adds more zaniness to the story, while Beatrice Lillie plays the villain, selling girls into "white slavery" under the guise of running a Chinese laundry. In the process, some entertaining songs are sung, none more memorable than the title song and "The Tapioca," along with some old standards such as "I Can't Believe That You're in Love with Me."

★BEST *of the* BEST★

☐ **OLIVER!** (1968)

The songs alone are enough to make this adaptation of Charles Dickens's classic novel *Oliver Twist* a great musical, but what is even more astonishing, given when it was made and that it was adapted from a Broadway play, is that its heart is never buried by its spectacle. For my part, "Food, Glorious Food," "Where Is Love?" "As Long as He Needs Me," "Who Will Buy?" and "Consider Yourself" are as enjoyable today as they were when the film came out. Little known fact: it was revealed many years after the film debuted that Mark Lester, who played Oliver, was dubbed by a twenty-four-year-old female singer named Kathe Green. Lester retired from acting to become an osteopath in England. This movie demonstrates once again that the best musicals are those that tackle a serious social issue—in this case, child exploitation.

Jack Wild and Mark Lester

☐ **CHITTY CHITTY BANG BANG** (1968)

Dick Van Dyke shines in this somewhat dated classic as the hapless inventor of a flying car. Loved by children not so much for specific songs as for the durability of its theme, its whimsical special effects and humor, and the inevitable happy ending, this one is a crowd pleaser, and not just for kids. Costar Sally Ann Howes tries her best not to imitate Julie Andrews, but it's Andrews you think of through the entire movie.

☐ **FINIAN'S RAINBOW** (1968)

Made twenty years too late and just as public interest in this type of musical was waning, the last feature film of the great Fred Astaire was not well received—by audiences or critics. When the show debuted as a Broadway play in 1947, it was a provocative look at racial strife in the American South, but the movie musical is so watered down that the plot seems almost irrelevant. The music, however, is timeless. Petula Clark costars as Astaire's daughter, singing the classics "How Are Things in Glocca Morra," "Look to the Rainbow," and "Old Devil Moon."

☐ **FUNNY GIRL** (1968) 🎭

One of the most popular movie musicals ever made, this comedy-drama is based on the career of comedienne Fanny Brice, with Barbra Streisand reprising her Broadway role. This is not a filmed stage play; it's a full-blown film drama with music. Brice's doomed relationship with gambler Nick Arnstein builds a tense plot through which "You Are Woman, I Am Man," "Don't Rain on My Parade," and other memorable songs are cleverly woven. One of Streisand's signature songs, "People," can be heard throughout the movie. Note how the restaging of the Ziegfeld Follies in the film set in the 1920s is anachronistically styled in the hairdos and eye makeup of the 1960s. Fanny Brice's self-effacing Jewish shtick is tempered to the taste of a new generation, and Streisand's closing rendition of Brice's classic "My Man" offers a whole new way of hearing the song. At the time, this was hailed as the part Streisand was born to play, and Hollywood being Hollywood, they had to make a sequel, *Funny Lady*, which concentrates on Brice's troubled relationship with Billy Rose. However well intentioned, the sequel doesn't really live up to the original, but it's worth a look just to hear Streisand sing "(It's Gonna Be a) Great Day" and "If I Love Again."

## ☐ STAR! (1968)

It's something of a mystery why this lavish musical, filled with songs by Noël Coward, Cole Porter, Kurt Weill, and George and Ira Gershwin did not fare very well at the box office. It is too long—that's probably one reason—but Julie Andrews is magnificent, singing comical music hall numbers as she climbs her way to the top in this fictionalized biography of the British stage legend Gertrude Lawrence, who rose from humble beginnings to become the toast of musical theater from 1912 to 1940. Daniel Massey is brilliant as Noël Coward. "Someone to Watch Over Me," "Limehouse Blues," and "Burlington Bertie from Bow" are enormously entertaining. Andrews herself calls this film "one of the last of the fabulously crafted Hollywood musicals." Her por-

★ BEST *of the* BEST ★

## ☐ HELLO, DOLLY! (1969)

An enormously successful Broadway play, *Hello, Dolly!* was brought to the motion picture screen with all the realism cinema can offer, beginning with the still photo that comes alive at the opening of the film. With direction by the master, Gene Kelly, choreography by Michael Kidd, and the finest screen performance of the legendary Louis Armstrong, this picture couldn't miss, and it doesn't. Some criticized Barbra Streisand as being too young (that must have been refreshing) for the part of Dolly Levi, a deal-making matchmaker in turn-of-the-century Yonkers, played on stage by Carol Channing, some twenty years her senior. As far as I'm concerned, Streisand pulls it off beautifully, and with her own voice. Look for echoes of Judy Garland singing "The Trolley Song" from *Meet Me in St. Louis* as Streisand and the chorus sing "Put On Your Sunday Clothes." (If you watch Disney's unusual 2008 animated film *WALL-E*, you'll hear the song again.) Not only are the sets lavish and authentic, it's the best use of Streisand's magnificent voice ever caught on screen. The film is also very funny. Says Dolly Levi, "If you are going to live from hand to mouth, you better be ambidextrous!" Costar Walter Matthau can't sing, but that never seems to bother anybody, since his main function in the film is to be cranky.

Michael Crawford and Barbra Streisand

trayal of Lawrence is spectacular, and when she shows her rougher edges, it's as if she really did get to be Eliza Doolittle after all.

### ☐ YELLOW SUBMARINE (1968) 🌞

This unique cartoon creation by the Beatles is a psychedelic journey to Pepperland, full of self-referential dialogue and in-jokes, none of which are necessary for children to know in order to follow the movie and get to know more than a dozen great Beatles songs.

### ☐ GOODBYE, MR. CHIPS (1969)

A music-added remake of the 1939 drama, this weeper stars Peter O'Toole, who can't sing, and Petula Clark, who definitely makes up for him. It's a mystery to me why anybody felt the need to remake this movie with music, since none of the songs seem to remain with you after the movie ends. What remains is the same emotional punch, having to do not with the music but with the love between the principal characters.

### ☐ PAINT YOUR WAGON (1969)

You'll either love it or hate it (sorry to say, I'm in the latter category), but the opportunity to see Clint Eastwood and Lee Marvin as singing cowboys is

Clint Eastwood in *Paint Your Wagon*

reason enough to watch this movie. Though the music is by the legendary Alan Jay Lerner and Frederick Loewe, with help from André Previn, the movie is nearly three hours long, which is enough to test anyone's patience. Set during the California Gold Rush and portraying the brawny men who worked the mines looking for wealth, this movie unfortunately does not offer a wealth of memorable tunes, with "They Call the Wind Maria" (pronounced "Mariah") and "I Talk to the Trees" being the best of them. The casting of the beautiful actress Jean Seberg in this movie is as perplexing as that of Eastwood and Marvin.

☐ **SWEET CHARITY** (1969)
Shirley MacLaine, Chita Rivera, Sammy Davis Jr., and Ricardo Montalban are among the stars who display their talents in this Broadway adaptation. Songs to listen for include "Rhythm of Life" and the unforgettable "If My Friends Could See Me Now." Despite all the feel-good singing and dancing around New York, this is a story about prostitution, and the point of view is alternately jaded and sentimental, with MacLaine leading us to believe that these are "the adventures of a girl who wanted to be loved," exposing us to some of the sillier aspects of the 1960s. It's hard to determine whether Charity is sweet or just plain stupid in this cynical story about a lying taxi dancer who shows her faith in the human race by hoping that romance will free her from her unsavory life. Bob Fosse directed the film, and its production numbers, particularly "Hey, Big Spender" with Rivera, are well worth your time. However, the film stands today as a flashy but soulless reminder of how hapless Hollywood was in creating memorable movies about the hippie era.

# DAYS NOT SO CLEAR
Civil Rights, the Sexual Revolution, and What to Sing About?

**1970s**

**M**USICALS BEGAN A PRECIPITOUS DECLINE IN THE 1970s. Hollywood simply did not know what to make of the sexual revolution and the social changes that were then taking place in America, resulting in preachy and pretentious musicals like *Hair* and *Jesus Christ Superstar*, with youth dancing around in drug-enhanced ecstasy.

These films led to nostalgia for the simpler 1950s, *Grease* being the best example. You will see in even the most successful musicals of the 1970s a sense of desperation and foreboding. *Cabaret*, arguably one of the best movie musicals of the decade, also harked back to another era for its theme, but in hindsight both *Cabaret* and *Grease* seem to lack a point of view. Were the 1930s a glorious age of sexual freedom or a monstrously decadent period that made Nazism unavoidable? Were the 1950s an age of innocence or repression?

Many of the most expensive productions of the decade seemed to be saying that more is better, but overdone films like *Darling Lili, Mame,* and *New York, New York,* which tried to mimic successful musicals of the past, bombed with the public. Instead, the 1970s gave us a wide selection of musical oddities that offer real insight into the mentality of the times and into Hollywood's inability to sing and dance the story of the social changes that were sweeping America.

## ☐ THE ARISTOCATS (1970) 

Alongside a good plotline involving greed, the super score of this animated Disney classic will get kids dancing and singing in no time. The familiar voices of Phil Harris, Sterling Holloway, and Maurice Chevalier can be heard, with the unforgettable voice of Eva Gabor as Duchess the cat.

## ☐ DARLING LILI (1970)

Lots of people have pronounced this film a failure. I, on the other hand, am so crazy about Julie Andrews that I have never seen a film with her in it that I didn't like. Her then-new husband Blake Edwards directed this box office flop, a very expensive spoof that casts Andrews as a World War I singer in London and Paris who is actually a spy for the Germans. Through the course of the film Andrews sings patriotic songs such as "Pack Up Your Troubles in Your Old Kit Bag and Smile, Smile, Smile!" and "It's a Long, Long Way to Tipperary." It's clear as the film unfolds that Edwards's tongue was firmly embedded in his cheek as he directed, but the viewing audience was changing and the film came along at just the wrong time. This is a visually gorgeous movie and the songs by Henry Mancini and Johnny Mercer include the superb opener "Whistling Away the Dark." Maybe the whole problem is our inability to accept Julie Andrews as a German spy, but when you think about it, what better cover could there be?

## ☐ ON A CLEAR DAY YOU CAN SEE FOREVER (1970)

Barbra Streisand singing the title song is perhaps reason enough to watch this kooky little film. But if that doesn't do it, "What Did I Have That I Don't Have?" might. Even though it's directed by the great Vincente Minnelli, this movie is uninspired and dated (not in a fun way). Streisand wears some great costumes in the dream sequence, but Yves Montand is miscast and dreadfully dull as her psychiatrist.

## ☐ SCROOGE (1970)

This retelling of Charles Dickens's novella *A Christmas Carol* puts a rather young (at thirty-four) but believable Albert Finney in the role of old Ebenezer

David Tomlinson, Angela Lansbury, Roy Snart, Cindy O'Callaghan, and Ian Weighill in *Bedknobs and Broomsticks*

*Scrooge*. This is a wonderful film to haul out year after year at Christmas and play for the entire family. "Thank You Very Much" is the most memorable song in a score that makes this one of the best musical retellings of a classic book. It's also fun to compare it to the 1992 retelling in which Kermit the Frog costars with Michael Caine, *The Muppet Christmas Carol*.

☐ **BEDKNOBS AND BROOMSTICKS** (1971)
The phenomenal Angela Lansbury is reason enough to see this movie. Although it never produced a hit song, it is a favorite of many who saw it as children. In "The Age of Not Believing," watching this "With a Flair" is "A Step in the Right Direction."

☐ **THE BOY FRIEND** (1971)
This homage to the 1920s has aged fairly well, mostly because the orchestration, sets, and costumes blend so well to create a sense of authenticity. Supermodel Twiggy does a rather good job in the film, singing and dancing to such standards as "You Are My Lucky Star" and "All I Do Is Dream of You," as well as a wealth of original tunes composed by Sandy Wilson. Unfortunately,

the film did not do well at the box office. It is interesting, however, to see how well Twiggy handles her first film, knowing how it bombed but still left her with an enduring career in fashion, music, and film. This is also the role that introduced Julie Andrews to American audiences on Broadway in 1954.

☐ **FIDDLER ON THE ROOF** (1971)

The songs "Sunrise, Sunset" and "If I Were a Rich Man" are so embedded in our national brain that it is essential to see the show in which they first entered our head. One of the most successful Broadway musicals ever, its transfer to film is authenticated by the filming locations (Yugoslavia posing as Ukraine) and the realistic approach to the time (1905 in Tsarist Russia). The music itself is a marvelous blend of Tin Pan Alley and Russian folk music style. Like all the best musicals, this one does not shy away from religion or ethnic conflict; similarly, it reinforces basic values of family, integrity, and morality. "Do You Love Me?" is one of the loveliest songs ever sung on film by two old lovers. What prevents this movie from being perfect is that at three hours it is simply too long, obscuring its message of simplicity and goodness.

☐ **WILLY WONKA AND THE CHOCOLATE FACTORY** (1971)

What I've always loved about Roald Dahl's children's books is that he has no patience with brats; they always get their comeuppance. Dahl wrote the screenplay for the film, the title of which was changed from *Charlie and the Chocolate Factory* to satisfy an ill-fated marketing campaign for a new chocolate bar. At any rate, the music and dancing all revolve around one poor little Charlie Bucket (played by Peter Östrum, who appeared in one movie and went on to become a veterinarian), who wins an opportunity to tour the most eccentric and wonderful candy factory of all, led by Gene Wilder in one of his best film roles. Memorable songs to listen for include "The Candy Man," "Pure Imagination," "Oompa-Loompa-Doompa-De-Do," and "I Want It Now!" sung with unabashed brattiness by Julie Dawn Cole. The film was remade in 2005 with Johnny Depp in the lead and retitled *Charlie and the Chocolate Factory*, like the original book.

☐ **LADY SINGS THE BLUES** (1972) 🔳

Diana Ross stars in this biographical film about the great singer Billie Holiday, who died in 1959. Although the film is clichéd and melodramatic in many ways, Ross rises above these shortcomings with a performance that captures the tragedy of Holiday's life and conveys the enormity of her singing

## ☐ CABARET (1972) 🎞

This is a very dark film, with dark choreography by the master of darkness, Bob Fosse. Joel Grey is brilliant as the emcee at the KitKat Club in 1931 Berlin, just as Nazism is taking hold. It was a freewheeling time, if we are to believe the film. The dancing girls all look like drug-addled whores and the customers are all titillation seekers in the smoky club. This all made for a good show on Broadway when the musical first appeared in 1966, and it makes for an even better film. *Cabaret* is Fosse's finest work simply because the choreography serves the story. Liza Minnelli as Sally Bowles, a lost American with a yen for fame and fortune and a talent for bad choices, gives an iconic performance, singing "Mein Herr" and the title song,

Liza Minnelli

soaking up the decadence, trying to be shocking, but ultimately revealing her vulnerability as she unwittingly enters a ménage à trois with Michael York and Helmut Griem, yielding some pretty titillating scenes for 1972. Much of what goes on in the club seems like a lesson in what made so many Germans embrace Hitler, as demonstrated by the chilling tune "Tomorrow Belongs to Me." But this is not history, this is drama with music, and it works together. Still a little scary after thirty years.

talent. There are many classics crammed into the film but none so well done as "Good Morning Heartache" and "God Bless the Child."

## ☐ MAN OF LA MANCHA (1972)

The reason to see this musical is to watch the gorgeous young Sophia Loren sing. The watching is more fun than the listening. When she is on screen, you just have to stare at her, in this otherwise overblown and confusing film that really is not much of a musical at all. Peter O'Toole is a great actor, but he cannot sing (and is not particularly well dubbed). The men in the chorus seem to know what they are doing, but none of the principals does any dancing. One

Joanne Jonas, Victor Garber, and Katie Hanley in *Godspell*

wonders what Miguel de Cervantes would make of this curious reinvention of his 1605 novel, *Don Quixote*.

☐ **1776** (1972)

Melding American history with a peculiarly American dramatic form, the musical comedy *1776* is a musical like no other, with actors playing founding fathers Benjamin Franklin, Thomas Jefferson, John Adams, and the entire Continental Congress. I often complain that I learned too much bogus history from the movies, but in this case, the movie makes history fun and stays true to the characters of our founding fathers according to the information about their personalities and quirks that has been handed down to us. Family viewing at its finest.

☐ **GODSPELL** (1973)

Even back in the 1970s, when skepticism reigned, the song "Day by Day" seemed like a genuine expression of reverence for the simple teachings of

Jesus Christ, despite the obvious efforts in this film to make him a psychedelic hero. While the hippie costumes and clown makeup don't hold up very well today, the point of the movie is to deliver a view of Christ as the radical threat to the status quo that he was. This film was part of an effort to make us take a new look at the gospels (see *Jesus Christ Superstar* as well) and make them relevant to contemporary life while avoiding any mention of sex, drugs, and rock and roll. Overall, it may seem naive and disingenuous now, but if you want a look at the antiestablishment, antimaterialism youth culture of the 1960s, this can't be beat.

## ☐ JESUS CHRIST SUPERSTAR (1973)

Filmed entirely in Israel, this reinterpretation of the stage rock opera is a good example of moviemaking in the 1970s. Told entirely in songs, images, and music, the story line focuses on the last days of Christ's life, his betrayal and crucifixion, as seen from the point of view of Judas, the disciple who betrayed him. Like *Godspell*, the film captures something, rather pretentiously, of the hippie mood of the times, as it begins with the cast unloading and assembling the set, then transitions trancelike into the time of Christ. In addition to the title song, other memorable moments by composer Andrew Lloyd Webber and lyricist Tim Rice to watch for include Yvonne Elliman singing "I Don't Know How to Love Him" and the group singing "Everything's Alright."

## ☐ THE LITTLE PRINCE (1974)

A science fiction musical based on a classic story by Antoine de Saint-Exupéry. How special is that? *The Little Prince* tells the magical story of an airplane pilot who makes a forced landing in the Sahara Desert, where he is befriended by a little prince from the planet Asteroid B-612. The pilot learns about the boy's history and planet-hopping journey, while the prince learns the secrets of the importance of life from a fox, a snake, and the pilot. The screenplay and lyrics by Alan Jay Lerner and music by Frederick Loewe mark one of the great creative team's last collaborations. Directed and produced by Stanley Donen, the film stars Steve Warner in the title role, with Richard Kiley as the aviator. Additional cast members include Bob Fosse (who choreographed his own dance sequence) and Gene Wilder. The desert sequences were filmed on location in Tunisia.

☐ **MAME** (1974)

Lucille Ball was not a singer. Her inability to sing was a running gag on her long-lived television show *I Love Lucy*. But Lucille Ball was a star, and she got her wish to headline in a musical when this Broadway show (featuring Angela Lansbury) was remade on film. This always begged to be a musical, which the highly successful 1958 film version, *Auntie Mame* with Rosalind Russell, was not. A lot of critics panned this film, saying that at sixty-three Ball was too old for the part and ridiculing the soft-focus lenses used for her close-ups, but don't listen to them. It's a lot of fun to watch, the sets are gorgeous, and the music is memorable. "We Need a Little Christmas" is a classic and should be hauled out every year ahead of "White Christmas." Lucy may not be a singer, but you can't take your eyes off her, and she is frequently very funny. It's said that Ball once quipped in defense of her singing in the film, "Mame stayed up all night and drank champagne! What did you expect her to sound like, Julie Andrews?" Robert Preston and Beatrice Arthur also give endearing performances, turning Mame into less of a nutcase and more of a lovable old broad.

☐ **AT LONG LAST LOVE** (1975)

Universally panned when it was released, this film was to have been director Peter Bogdanovich's tribute to the great musicals of the 1930s. Instead, it was reviled and a box office flop. I suspect this had to do with changing tastes and the disfavor the director and star Cybill Shepherd were experiencing at the time. Bogdanovich himself admitted that his technique of recording the songs live as the numbers were filmed was a mistake. Years later, Woody Allen tried the same sort of homage with *Everyone Says I Love You* (1996), to a much better reception. Still, with sixteen Cole Porter songs to hear, I'd rather watch this than a rock opera any day.

☐ **LISZTOMANIA** (1975)

Roger Daltrey, lead singer of the rock group the Who, stars in this sendup of the imagined bawdy life of composer Franz Liszt, his friendship with Richard Wagner, and his affairs with multiple mistresses. If you have already discovered *Hedwig and the Angry Inch* or *The Rocky Horror Picture Show*, you must give this one a try. "Over the top" is the expression many reviewers use to describe it.

☐ **NASHVILLE** (1975) ▓▓▓

If you can suffer through director Robert Altman's homage to (or is it ridicule of?) country music, perhaps you can explain why this movie is considered great by so many people. I consider it boring and realistic in ways that I never want my musicals to be. The music seems improvised on the spot—and much of it apparently was. Even the Oscar winner "I'm Easy" is a real snoozer.

☐ **THE ROCKY HORROR PICTURE SHOW** (1975) ▓▓▓

This odd film has become a cult classic. To understand why, you have to know that it was something of a flop when it first came out, but it got picked up at late-night screenings on college campuses, and audiences started dressing up as characters in the film, throwing rice and toast at the screen during appropriate moments, talking back to the characters, and just generally turning the screening into a party. What the partying did was make hard rock, sadomasochism, and homoerotic innuendo palatable to the moviegoing public. Still, knowing the great roles that were to follow, it's fun to watch the young Susan Sarandon as the innocent ingenue.

☐ **TOMMY** (1975)

From the beginning, I sided with those who found *Tommy* to be insufferably pretentious and (the worst sin of all) boring. It is contrived hippie excess at its most typical, and I just don't remember anything in the film resonating with real life. The fact that it was being marketed as a rock opera perplexed me even more. In the face of peer pressure to like it, I just kept my mouth shut. Truth be told, the reason to see this film is neither for the music nor for the stars; no, the real reason is to see how moviemakers' perceptions of reality wind up making a better social studies course than entertainment.

☐ **THE FIRST NUDIE MUSICAL** (1976)

If you remember and loved Cindy Williams in *Laverne and Shirley*, this movie is for you—but don't expect to see her naked. Stephen Nathan costars as the heir to a Hollywood studio forced to make a musical comedy porno film. The movie feels low budget and employs the classic musical-within-a-movie premise, but with a lot of sexual humor: the musical features such songs as "Orgasm," "Lesbian, Butch, Dyke," and "Dancing Dildos." It's an unusual film, with something of a cult following who find it hilarious. Curiosity is the main reason to see it.

## ☐ NEW YORK, NEW YORK (1977)

This movie is ambitious in so many ways that some of them were bound to fail. Yet watching it fail is at least interesting, directed as it is by Martin Scorsese, who has a little trouble with the concept of a musical. Robert De Niro is thoroughly dislikable as the egotistical saxophone player who somehow falls head over heels for Liza Minnelli, playing a lounge singer who is at first resistant to his obvious shortcomings but then becomes the victim of them. About two hours into their marital problems and you'll probably have had enough, but the re-creation of post–World War II America and the collection of great songs that get sung during the course of the movie are terrific, including the now-famous title tune. Minnelli sings some classics: "Once in a While," "You Are My Lucky Star," "The Man I Love," and "Just You, Just Me." One way to have made the movie shorter would have been to cut the unbearable "But the World Goes 'Round." Take special note of sexy Diahnne Abbott, De Niro's first wife in real life, performing "Honeysuckle Rose" in one of the nightclub scenes.

## ☐ SATURDAY NIGHT FEVER (1977) 🎞

Because this movie is so good, the "disco sucks" crowd has never wanted to admit that they liked it, or in some cases have never even seen it. The Bee

John Travolta in *Saturday Night Fever*

Gees (Barry, Maurice, and Robin Gibb) and other disco singers provide the soundtrack to John Travolta's superb portrayal of a swaggering sexy guy from Brooklyn who takes up with a girl from Manhattan. The drama is honest, Travolta's performance is spot-on, and the songs sound better today than ever: "How Deep Is Your Love," "If I Can't Have You," "More Than a Woman," "Night Fever," "Stayin' Alive," "You Should Be Dancing"—they all convey a real sense of what it was like spinning around on the dance floor under that disco ball.

☐ **AMERICAN HOT WAX** (1978)
Tim McIntire stars in this difficult to find biopic loosely based on the life of Cleveland disc jockey Alan Freed, who introduced rock and roll to teenage American radio listeners in the 1950s.

☐ **THE BUDDY HOLLY STORY** (1978)
Gary Busey portrays rock and roll legend Buddy Holly, whose promising career and life were cut short in a plane crash. Busey performs some of Holly's greatest hits, including "Peggy Sue" and "Whole Lotta Shakin' Goin' On."

☐ **THANK GOD IT'S FRIDAY** (1978)
The quintessential disco movie, starring the queen of disco, Donna Summer (who was a very good singer, incidentally), this flick does what it sets out to do—it delivers a fun time. I don't remember seeing it when it came out; I figured I would skip the movie and just go to a disco for the experience. Now, the film just reminds me how really danceable those songs by Summer, the Commodores, Giorgio Moroder, Thelma Houston, and the Village People were. Why do you think people in health clubs still favor disco over rock for dancercise?

☐ **THE WIZ** (1978)
It's kind of a shame that this movie isn't better. There's certainly enough talent here to have made it glorious, and what an interesting idea to remake *The Wizard of Oz* with an all-black cast. But talent and an idea are not enough. Diana Ross is stuck with trying to make us believe in a mousy thirty-five-year-old Dorothy. Although he sure can dance, Michael Jackson is more pitiful than playful as the Scarecrow. Even Lena Horne, Nipsey Russell, and Richard Pryor can't quite make the thing work. The music is oddly uninspired, but not surprisingly, Mabel King as the Wicked Witch really wakes

you up with "Don't Nobody Bring Me No Bad News." "Ease on Down the Road" is probably the song you will remember when the movie is over, but because this movie is such an oddity, you really must see it—or at least watch clips on YouTube.

★BEST *of the* BEST★

## ☐ GREASE (1978)

Following a great run on stage, this film adaption features Olivia Newton-John and John Travolta at just the ages (Newton-John was thirty, Travolta twenty-four) at which they could play teenagers and get away with it, and much of the movie's success hinged on their appeal singing songs like "Summer Nights" and "Hopelessly Devoted to You" (my personal favorite). Of course, realism is never the point in a musical; the point is romance and fantasy and looking at something in a new way. It has always amazed me that science fiction fans can believe almost anything—walking on Mars, invaders from Venus—but they cannot believe a simple romantic fantasy. The title song, performed by Frankie Valli, is a signature song of the last half of the twentieth century. This movie represents in one very special way a stretch of Hollywood history that seems pretty obscure in the twenty-first century. Joan Blondell appears in this film as a sympathetic waitress; keep in mind this is the actress who delivered "Remember My Forgotten Man" in *Gold Diggers of 1933*. "Beauty School Dropout" sung by Frankie Avalon is memorable, as is film legend Eve Arden as the clueless principal delivering the line, "If you can't be an athlete, be an athletic supporter." *Grease* is the musical that sums up the repressive, nasty, ignorant, terrific 1950s. There was also a *Grease 2* four years later, which you will want to check out if *Grease* does it for you, but it was generally panned. John Travolta is arguably the best all-around actor-singer-dancer of the last half of the twentieth century.

Olivia Newton-John and John Travolta

## ☐ ALL THAT JAZZ (1979) 🎞 📷

There is nothing romantic about this film depicting the struggles of the great choreographer Bob Fosse, as portrayed by Roy Scheider and as directed by Fosse himself. The marketing hype for the film proclaimed it a "masterwork," and the Academy of Motion Picture Arts and Sciences lavished Oscars on it, but it is painful to watch, as it exposes the backstage struggles of countless music wannabes who mask their disappointments with smiles and drugs. Memorable numbers include "On Broadway" and "Everything Old Is New Again." But this is not so much a musical as a cynical, often surreal drama about the narcissistic people who make musical theater. Sorry, but this one is not for the kids (it's raunchy, and they would probably be bored silly).

## ☐ HAIR (1979)

I remember liking the song "Aquarius" from *Hair* after the Fifth Dimension covered it in a thoroughly singable version. I had seen the musical on stage in 1968 and remember feeling that it seemed like an effort to capitalize on the antiwar movement and to dilute its message. With hair hanging past my shoulders, I was embarrassed that the show seemed to be saying that the best way to express rebellion was to take off your clothes. Ten years later when the movie came out, the show seemed completely redundant. But now I am glad that we have this film version of the sexual revolution that points out more than anything how superficial impressions of an era are formed from popular entertainment—and how they endure. While songs like "Sodomy" and "Hashish" may have made audiences feel daring and hip in the '60s, most of the music and the posturing do not stand the test of time very well.

More Entertaining Than Humanly Possible!

## ☐ THE MUPPET MOVIE (1979)

🎞 What's not to love about this classic? "Rainbow Connection" is as fresh today as the day it was written and will forever be associated with Jim Henson as the voice of Kermit the Frog, who is on a trek across America with his new friends seeking success in Hollywood. For more great family viewing, try *The Great Muppet Caper* (1981) and *The Muppets Take Manhattan* (1984).

## ☐ QUADROPHENIA (1979)

The movie trailer called this "The Who's triumphant answer to indifference." Set in London in 1965, this rock opera assembles an array of young British acting talents (including Sting) who act as London's 1960s mods and rockers against the soundtrack of the Who's 1973 album *Quadrophenia*, marketed as a "concept album." Phil Daniels plays drug-addled Jimmy, who hates his job and is misunderstood by his parents. Watching his downward spiral into paranoia and isolation is no pleasure, and if you are young it will make you glad you missed the '60s.

## ☐ THE ROSE (1979)

*The Rose* tells of the tragic life of a self-destructive female rock star, modeled after Janis Joplin and played by Bette Midler in her most serious dramatic role. Through the course of this relentlessly depressing tale, Midler sings some great songs: "Midnight in Memphis," "When a Man Loves a Woman," and the gut-wrenching title song.

# ANYTHING GOES

## Fame and the Me Generation

1980s

**A**FTER THE 1970S, MOVIE MUSICALS MOVED AWAY from social issues almost entirely and toward a me-centered posture that gave us *Fame* and *Flashdance*. My nomination for the best musical of the decade, however, goes to *Yentl*. Critics have been harsh on Barbra Streisand, but her giant talent is more apparent in this film than any other. Streisand wisely presents most of the music in *Yentl* as voice-over, so no one jumps up from the dinner table and starts singing. This technique gives a rather preposterous story believability, like a fairy tale.

In the midst of other me-centered fare such as Prince's *Purple Rain* and John Travolta in *Staying Alive* comes the delightful musical comedy *Victor/Victoria*, the long-awaited showcase for the talents of a mature Julie Andrews, and the film is just plain fun to watch.

## ☐ THE BLUES BROTHERS (1980)

There's plenty of music in this comedy spin-off from a *Saturday Night Live* TV skit with Dan Aykroyd and John Belushi, in which Jake Blues and his brother Elwood put together a band to save the Catholic home in Chicago where they were raised. In addition to some fine numbers by the brothers, this movie features plenty of classics: "Hold On! I'm a Comin'," by Sam and Dave; "Think," performed by Aretha Franklin; "I'm Walkin'," by Fats Domino; and "Jailhouse Rock," performed by the Blues Brothers with Franklin, James Brown, Cab Calloway, and Ray Charles.

☐ **CAN'T STOP THE MUSIC** (1980) 🔳
Somebody should have stopped the music early in this film and decided just what the point was. Without ever mentioning the word "gay," it is one of the gayest movies ever made, yet it never stops pandering to straight audiences by focusing on star Valerie Perrine's cleavage. Ostensibly the tale of the formation and rise to fame of the disco group the Village People, the movie will leave you forever wondering how "YMCA" became an anthem at major macho sports events. Mesmerizing as a car wreck.

☐ **COAL MINER'S DAUGHTER** (1980) 🔳
Sissy Spacek is absolutely spectacular as country singer Loretta Lynn, and Tommy Lee Jones is unforgettable in the role of her husband. The part won Spacek an Oscar for best actress. This may be one of the best biopics ever, largely because it concentrates on an authentic rendering of Lynn's life story, rather than on the country-western music she sings.

☐ **FAME** (1980)
This film follows the lives of several teenagers who attend a New York high school for students gifted in the performing arts. It stars Irene Cara, who sings a number of memorable hits, including the title tune and "Out Here on My Own." The cast's rendering of "I Sing the Body Electric" is also notable. This movie is often said to have ushered in the self-centered youth culture of the 1980s. I don't give it that much credit, but it does mark the coming of age of Generation X. Movies, especially musicals, rarely usher in social movements; rather, they reflect them long after they are faits accomplis. In 2009, MGM released an updated and blander version of life at the same school by the same title and featuring the title tune as a curtain call.

☐ **URBAN COWBOY** (1980)
Debra Winger and John Travolta engage in mechanical bull riding and country dancing in Houston, on the bumpy road to love. Though not a musical

Sissy Spacek, Minnie Pearl, and Ernest Tubb in *Coal Miner's Daughter*

per se, the songs in this contemporary Western are a feast for those who like country music; if you don't, the story is pretty good, too. Along the way, you get to hear "Hello Texas," performed by Jimmy Buffett; "All Night Long," by Joe Walsh; "Times like These," by Dan Fogelberg; "Don't It Make Ya Wanna Dance," performed by Bonnie Raitt; "Look What You've Done to Me," by Boz Scaggs; "Love the World Away," by Kenny Rogers; and "Mammas Don't Let Your Babies Grow Up to Be Cowboys," by Mickey Gilley and Johnny Lee, among many others on the soundtrack.

## ☐ **XANADU** (1980)

Often cited as one of the worst musicals ever made, this movie gets a bad rap for being corny and a big fat cliché. What is lost on critics is that it is an absolute hoot to watch, being both entertaining and deliberately over the top. How could I not want to watch my all-time dancing idol Gene Kelly, looking great at sixty-eight and cavorting around with Olivia Newton-John? Their fantasy dance with her in uniform is lovely.

☐ **PENNIES FROM HEAVEN** (1981)

Set in Chicago during the Great Depression and filled with great songs from that era, this is an imaginative picture, in which most of the songs are mimed by the film's stars Steve Martin (as a traveling sheet music salesman) and Bernadette Peters (a teacher who works in a sheet music store), as they escape the desperation of their lives and their illicit affair in a fantasy world taken from the silver screen. Christopher Walken's dance to "Let's Misbehave" is not to be missed. This is a strange and strangely compelling film, with Martin in an unusual role.

☐ **ANNIE** (1982)

Try as she might, Carol Burnett simply cannot get us to dislike her enough as the nasty Miss Hannigan in this adaptation of a wildly popular Broadway musical based on the comic strip *Little Orphan Annie*. No matter, this musical is beautifully made, with a first-rate cast that also includes Albert Finney as Daddy Warbucks, Ann Reinking, Tim Curry, and Bernadette Peters—and (spoiler alert) Hannigan has a heart of gold, anyway. Aileen Quinn as Annie really belts out the showstopping best song in the film, "Tomorrow."

☐ **THE BEST LITTLE WHOREHOUSE IN TEXAS** (1982)

Adapted for the screen from a successful Broadway play of the same name, this film did not go down well with movie audiences, despite the charms of Dolly Parton, Burt Reynolds, and a talent-riddled cast. Parton performs "I Will Always Love You," a song she wrote that was later made more popular by Whitney Houston. There's something a bit forced about the humor, but it is interesting as a musical with a big heart.

☐ **LA TRAVIATA** (1982)

Director Franco Zeffirelli brings Giuseppe Verdi's opera gloriously to the screen with a cast that includes Teresa Stratas, Plácido Domingo, and Cornell MacNeil, as well as the Metropolitan Opera orchestra and chorus, in this Oscar-nominated production. This might be a good opera to watch after Bizet's *Carmen*, if you are trying to understand the musical form.

☐ **PINK FLOYD: THE WALL** (1982)

This is a must-see musical only if you are a fan of Pink Floyd and love the hard rock of the 1960s—oh, and if you are in the mood to watch a troubled rock star descend into madness.

## ☐ VICTOR/VICTORIA (1982)

Julie Andrews has never been better than in this farce, playing a woman pretending to be a man pretending to be a woman. Safely set in 1934 Paris, this film makes great use of James Garner, who unwittingly falls for the charms of Victoria before he knows that she is a he—except she's really not. Lesley Ann Warren delivers one of the best dumb blondes in cinema history as the bimbo who is in love with Garner, and Robert Preston steals the show—well, some of it—singing "Shady Dame from Seville" in drag. This musical is unusual for having taken the reverse route, beginning as a film and then becoming a successful Broadway play. It's a triumph for Andrews and her director-husband Blake Edwards. Fortunately, it does not take itself too seriously, and by the end everyone is laughing, having fallen nearly completely out of character. The incomparable Henry Mancini wrote the music for the film, and it is beautifully integrated into the story line.

## ☐ FLASHDANCE (1983)

Lovely Jennifer Beals plays a young woman who is a steelworker by day, an exotic dancer by night. Her dream is to get into a real dance company, and with encouragement from her boss-boyfriend, she may get her chance. The

Jennifer Beals in *Flashdance*

★ BEST *of the* BEST ★

## ☐ YENTL (1983)

The beauty of *Yentl* is the way the music and the story are woven together, often with voice-over rather than people bursting into song for no appar-

Barbra Streisand

ent reason (something that always seems to bother people who hate musicals). This film is Barbra Streisand's crowning achievement, as star and director, and with music composed by Michel Legrand, it's sublime. Based on a short story by Isaac Bashevis Singer, the film is set in Poland and takes us back to a time when the Holocaust had not happened and girls who passed themselves off as boys were pretty much viewed as demons. This movie musical works on every level, from the scenery to the voices. Seamlessly woven into the plot are the lovely songs "Papa, Can You Hear Me?" "Where Is It Written," "The Way He Makes Me Feel," "Will Someone Ever Look at Me That Way?" and "A Piece of Sky."

city of Pittsburgh costars. There is plenty of music in *Flashdance*, but none as memorable as the title song performed by Irene Cara. What a feeling! And who can forget that exhilarating scene in which Beals is doused with water, or the one in which she dances to "Maniac"? Never mind that Beals's best dance scenes were done with a body double; this is still a worthy film for young people with terpsichorean dreams.

## ☐ STAYING ALIVE (1983)

This is a fine example of just how narcissistic the 1980s got; it stars John Travolta in a sort of musical *Rocky* and was directed by none other than Sylvester Stallone. It's full of meaningless and often hilarious posturing—a study in mediocrity. Travolta at the height of his youthful sexiness can neither save this film from its own cynicism nor redeem his character from his antiromantic excess and self-involvement. Barely a musical, it does peak with Travolta and

Cynthia Rhodes's elegant dance to "I'm Never Gonna Give You Up," which you can see on YouTube without having to suffer through the entire movie.

## ☐ AMADEUS (1984) 🔳

Tom Hulce is wacky and sensational as composer Wolfgang Amadeus Mozart in this stylish and enormously popular biopic. F. Murray Abraham delivers a flawless performance as the envious rival Antonio Salieri. Of course it takes liberties with history, but that is what a movie is supposed to do. It's the beautiful music of Mozart throughout the film that makes *Amadeus* so memorable. The opera scenes were choreographed by the legendary Twyla Tharp and are something to behold.

## ☐ CARMEN (1984)

One of the truly great film adaptations of an opera, Bizet's *Carmen* succeeds where others fail because it is pure cinema. Filmed entirely in Andalusian Spain, the authentic scenery and sets capture what it must have been like to be alive in nineteenth-century Seville, even though composer Georges Bizet never visited Spain. The authentic Spanish feel of the film is even more amazing given that the entire opera is in French. The performances by Plácido Domingo, Julia Migenes, and every one of the dozens of singers and dancers who populate the film are flawless. "The Toreador Song" will linger with you forever. This is the opera-hater's opera.

## ☐ THE COTTON CLUB (1984)

Even though it is certainly the definitive film take on New York's famed Cotton Club of the 1920s, this film suffers because the story line bogs it down instead of pulling it along. And why, one wonders, more than forty years after *Cabin in the Sky*, does Hollywood still need the white story line and the relegation of black performers to specialty numbers? In many ways the film re-creates the segregation of the times in which it is set. While individual performances are stunning, one senses that despite the writing power behind the script—William Kennedy, Francis Ford Coppola, Mario Puzo—the thing was written by a committee that could not decide if it wanted to make a crime flick or a musical. At two hours and nine minutes, the film sometimes begs for fast-forward, past the gangster banter to the songs, especially the performance of the multi-talented Gregory Hines. The scenes in the Cotton Club are exhilarating and give some sense of what it must have been like at the height of its racially segregated popularity. Hines and his brother Maurice Hines do a tap dance number in a manner that suggests the legendary Nicholas Brothers. Broadway legend Gwen Verdon as the mother adds another touch of magic. The scene with Hines and Lonette McKee in the Hoofers Club is worth its weight in gold. Ultimately the blood bath wins out—and that's *not* entertainment.

## ☐ FOOTLOOSE (1984)

This classic starring Kevin Bacon (he of the "six degrees of separation") is filled with hit songs, such as the title track and "Let's Hear It for the Boy." It's a must-see for its clever combination of dance choreography with the touching story of a teenager who moves from Chicago to a small town in the West where rock music and dancing are illegal.

## ☐ PURPLE RAIN (1984)

As the first starring film role for the singer once again known as Prince, this glorified music video contains a catalog of Prince's hit songs, including the title song, "When Doves Cry," "I Would Die 4 U," and "Let's Go Crazy." Between songs is the story of a singer's miserable home life at the hands of a brutal father, played rather well by Clarence Williams III. Apollonia Kotero costars. This musical is not so different from musicals of thirty or forty years earlier that served as a showcase for the talents of the star and the hit tunes rather than as a film on its own merits.

## ☐ THIS IS SPINAL TAP (1984) ▦

Something of a cult classic, this movie is treasured by many as the final hilarious word on rock documentaries, lame rock groups, inflated rocker egos, and self-important rock hangers-on. Directed by Rob Reiner (Meathead on TV's *All in the Family*), this film has never moved me one way or the other, but with satire, you have to know and care about the original to get the joke.

## ☐ A CHORUS LINE (1985)

This great Broadway musical seems somehow deflated on the big screen. The secret of the play's success was the up-close and personal insight into each of the aspiring performer's hopes, dreams, and fears. But unless a revival is coming to a theater near you, watch this cinematic version imagining that you are seeing it live. Several of the songs are knockouts, especially "One" and "What I Did for Love." Listen to his voice as Michael Douglas auditions the players as the director.

Ann Wedgeworth and Jessica Lange in *Sweet Dreams*

☐ **SWEET DREAMS** (1985) 

In this stunningly underappreciated biopic, Jessica Lange shines as country singer Patsy Cline, whose life was cut short when she was killed in a plane crash at age thirty. She left behind some memorable songs, including "Crazy" and "I Fall to Pieces." This is another biopic in which the star, Lange, lip-synchs to recordings of the original artist.

☐ **WHITE NIGHTS** (1985)

It's a shame that a film starring two brilliant dancers—Mikhail Baryshnikov and Gregory Hines—with choreography by the legendary Twyla Tharp, backed up by acting giants Geraldine Page, Helen Mirren, and Isabella Rossellini, isn't better. Part of the problem is that it doesn't know what it wants to be—it's not a musical in any traditional sense, yet the only scenes that are truly successful are the dance sequences. Still it's interesting to watch as a film about the Cold War and to see the way it parallels Baryshnikov's own defection from the Soviet Union a decade earlier. The film is also notable for the Academy Award–winning song "Say You, Say Me" by Lionel Richie, as well as "Separate Lives," performed by Phil Collins and Marilyn Martin.

☐ **ABSOLUTE BEGINNERS** (1986)

The main attraction here is the score, which features the title song and "That's Motivation," composed and performed by rock icon David Bowie, as well as his version of the old standard "Volare." In addition, you get "Killer Blow" performed by Sade and jazz tunes by Charles Mingus and Miles Davis performed by Gil Evans. This movie makes you believe that if David Bowie had been performing in the 1950s, he would have been a sensation then too.

☐ **LABYRINTH** (1986)

A teenage girl, played by Jennifer Connelly, gets her wish when the Goblin King, played by David Bowie, takes her baby brother off to his castle to be goblinized, forcing her to travel through the labyrinth to rescue him. This enchanting feature is notable for Jim Henson's Muppet creations interacting with the live actors and for its impressive production values and art design. The interesting soundtrack is loaded with songs by Bowie, who has always loved to combine a little science fiction with his rock and roll. This peek into the mind of a rock icon is a great "be careful what you wish for" movie, perfect for young adults.

☐ **LITTLE SHOP OF HORRORS** (1986)

There isn't much truly memorable music in this adaptation of the stage play, but comedian Rick Moranis is entertaining as Seymour, a nerd working in a flower shop who grows a very unusual plant indeed, thereby immortalizing the line "Feed me, Seymour."

☐ **SID AND NANCY** (1986)

Gary Oldman and Chloe Webb play punk rockers Sid Vicious and Nancy Spungen, whose drug addictions led to Spungen's death and Vicious's arrest for murder. It's a morbid tale, but it offers a lot of insight into the culture of sex, drugs, and rock and roll that made Vicious's band the Sex Pistols so popular with so many.

☐ **DIRTY DANCING** (1987)

No list of must-see musicals would be complete without the most treasured romantic film of the 1980s, the one in which Patrick Swayze and Jennifer Grey set the new standard for sexiness. If you saw Grey—who is *Cabaret's* Joel Grey's daughter, by the way—on the 2010 season of TV's *Dancing with*

Patrick Swayze and Jennifer Grey in *Dirty Dancing*

*the Stars*, you know that she has not lost a thing in the quarter century that has passed since this film first touched romantic hearts all over America. Watch them dance to "The Time of My Life" as sung by Bill Medley and Jennifer Warnes and sigh.

☐ **LA BAMBA** (1987) 📷

Ritchie Valens was a singer, songwriter, and guitarist who died at eighteen in the same plane crash that killed fellow musicians Buddy Holly and J. P. "The Big Bopper" Richardson in 1959. His recording career lasted a mere eight months, yet he scored several hits, most notably the title tune, and he was a true pioneer of Latin rock and roll. Lou Diamond Phillips stars in this must-see biopic.

☐ **BEACHES** (1988)

A privileged rich girl, played by Barbara Hershey, and a struggling entertainer, played by Bette Midler, share a turbulent but strong childhood friendship over the years, the ups and downs of which are the core of this melodrama. The reason to see it is the soundtrack with Bette Midler in top voice performing a lot of great songs, including "Under the Boardwalk," Cole

Porter's "I've Still Got My Health," and Randy Newman's brilliant "I Think It's Going to Rain Today," all of which I like better than the sappy "Wind Beneath My Wings." Sorry.

☐ **BIRD** (1988) 📷

Biopics don't get much better than this one, in which Forest Whitaker impersonates jazz musician Charlie "Bird" Parker to a tee. Directed by Clint Eastwood, this film is essential for anyone who loves jazz or wants learn more about jazz and the tortured souls who created the best of it.

☐ **GREAT BALLS OF FIRE** (1989) 📷

Dennis Quaid rocks as Jerry Lee Lewis, one of rock and roll's all time great naughty boys. Lewis himself provides the vocals, while Quaid captures the energy and irreverence of the performance where there is a "Whole Lotta Shakin' Goin' On."

☐ **THE LITTLE MERMAID** (1989) 🎞

A mermaid princess makes a Faustian bargain with an unscrupulous sea hag in order to meet a human prince on land. This Disney favorite features an unusual heroine and atypical music, such as the favorite "Under the Sea" reggae tune.

# DOWNTRODDEN AND MISUNDERSTOOD
Boys, Bodyguards, and Ballroom Dancing

**1990s**

Y NOMINATION FOR THE BEST MUSICAL OF THIS slim-pickings decade goes to *Evita* and its political realism. Critics have been loath to admit that Madonna is mesmerizing in this film. When you watch *Evita*, keep in mind that this is a movie without dialogue. The fact that it is based on a stage play makes it that much more impressive because of its complete adaptation to the film medium. It's visually stunning, intense, and electrifying, like an opera.

The other big development that marks the 1990s is the release of *Beauty and the Beast*, which injected new life into animated musicals and created a new kind of heroine for young girls—one whose nose was always in a book and whose Prince Charming was anything but. After you've seen the movie you will never be able to hear "Beauty and the Beast" again without hearing Angela Lansbury's unmistakable voice singing it.

☐ **BEAUTY AND THE BEAST** (1991) ▦ ☀

*Broadway* magazine said this "brilliant" film "started a revolution of sorts." Based on the classic story, the heroine, Belle, is a nontraditional princess, an intelligent woman who is always reading and is not seeking her Prince Charming. This film also demonstrates a new Computer Animation Production System developed by Disney and especially evident in the ballroom scene. The incomparable Angela Lansbury sings the equally unforgettable title song.

## ☐ THE COMMITMENTS (1991)

The book on which the film is based, the film itself, and the soundtrack were hugely popular after the movie was released; some of the film's actors were still touring years afterward. This comedy drama set in Dublin tells the story of "the world's hardest working band" as it struggles to bring soul music to the people of the city.

## ☐ THE DOORS (1991) 📷

Val Kilmer chews up the scenery as ego-maniacal rock and roll star Jim Morrison, lead singer of the Doors. If you have heard "Light My Fire" and want to know more about what made this man so charismatic that forty years after his death mourners are still drawn to his grave in Père-Lachaise cemetery in Paris, this biopic is a must.

Bronagh Gallagher, Angeline Ball, Maria Doyle Kennedy, and Andrew Strong in *The Commitments*

☐ **FOR THE BOYS** (1991)

Bette Midler finally gets the role she was born to play in this comedy-drama in which she and James Caan are entertainers during World War II. Something about this film tested the patience of audiences—it's too long, for one thing—and they stayed away in droves. I thoroughly enjoy Midler's energetic performance, and there are so many great songs to hear—"I'll Walk Alone," "I Remember You," "The More I See You," "For All We Know," and "P.S. I Love You" among them. My favorite John Lennon/Paul McCartney song is "In My Life," and it's never been done better than by the Divine Miss M.

☐ **ALADDIN** (1992) 🎞

The voice of Robin Williams as the genie stands out in this retelling of the classic tale about Aladdin, who falls in love with Princess Jasmine but cannot marry her because she can only marry a prince. The lovely song "A Whole New World" is one of many that enrich the film. The lesson: be careful what you wish for, you might get it.

☐ **THE BODYGUARD** (1992)

Whitney Houston became a movie star in this film, which offers a lot of insight into the level of talent and appeal she had some twenty years before her untimely death in 2012. Although this is not a musical per se (more of a romantic thriller), Houston plays a pop singer and performs, among other songs, her signature tune, "I Will Always Love You," which was written by country music legend Dolly Parton.

☐ **MAMBO KINGS** (1992)

Starring Antonio Banderas and Armand Assante as Cuban brothers in a mambo band in the 1950s, *Mambo Kings* is really a celebration of Latin American music. This underrated film has both a compelling story and a soundtrack that features over twenty songs performed by the likes of Los Lobos, Linda Ronstadt, and Celia Cruz. You even get to hear the great Jo Stafford classic "You Belong to Me."

☐ **NEWSIES** (1992)

This musical is based on the New York City newsboy strike of 1899, when young newspaper sellers stood up to their ruthless, exploitative bosses. Disney produced this tough precursor to television musicals in which young people burst into songs largely related to their own angst. The young men who perform in this musical are nothing short of astonishing. This is a musical in the truest sense: the songs tell the story. Ann-Margret, often underappreciated as an actress, shines in the small role of Medda Larkson. You will look into the faces of these self-described "bunch of street rats" and wonder how such performances are made to happen—and wonder even more about the real boys who inspired them. Although this show never produced any "hit tunes" of note, "The World Will Know" and "Seize the Day" stand out as the best songs in the film. Watch carefully and you'll spot a young Christian Bale in the cast.

☐ **SISTER ACT** (1992)
A lot of fun to watch, if completely unrealistic, this tale has the hilarious Whoopi Goldberg playing a lounge singer who is being stalked by the mob. If that isn't ridiculous enough, the authorities concoct a scheme to hide her in a convent. There, she ends up transforming the dull choir into a band of rockin' sisters. Kathy Najimy is hilarious, as is the ubiquitous Maggie Smith as Mother Superior. The topper has to be their rendition of "My Guy," the 1960s Mary Wells hit for Motown. The movie was such a hit that a less successful follow-up, *Sister Act 2: Back in the Habit*, was released a year later.

☐ **STRICTLY BALLROOM** (1992)
Lots of dancing makes this Australian gem a must, especially for fans of ballroom dancing. The soundtrack is a cornucopia of music types, from Cyndi Lauper's "Time after Time" to Bizet's *Carmen*.

☐ **THE NIGHTMARE BEFORE CHRISTMAS** (1993)
The strange world created by writer Tim Burton and composer Danny Elfman is actually a combination of Halloween and Christmas—a dream come true for children, or rather, a nightmare come true. The music is engaging, the characters intriguing; this has become a classic that continues to delight audiences year after year.

☐ **SWING KIDS** (1993)
This story of a group of young people who listen to forbidden music in Nazi Germany is not really a musical, yet it contains more than a dozen songs, some of the best music of the World War II era, including Count Basie's "Jumpin' at the Woodside," Duke Ellington's "It Don't Mean a Thing (If It

Ain't Got That Swing)," "You Go to My Head," and "Swingtime in the Rock-
ies," performed by Benny Goodman.

☐ **WHAT'S LOVE GOT TO DO WITH IT** (1993) 🔲
Angela Bassett turns in a great performance as popular singer Tina Turner,
and Laurence Fishburne is equally effective as her abusive husband, Ike.

☐ **IMMORTAL BELOVED** (1994) 🔲
Gary Oldman stars as composer Ludwig van Beethoven in this biopic that
attempts to uncover the "immortal beloved," an otherwise unidentified
woman to whom Beethoven wrote a love letter that was never sent. While
critics were not particularly kind to this movie, the soundtrack is like listening to Beethoven's greatest hits, and what's wrong with that?

☐ **THE LION KING** (1994) 🔆
A breakthrough for Disney, this movie is set in Africa and the main character
is a prince—instead of a princess—who is tricked into thinking he killed his
father and flees into exile. The music is a collaboration between Elton John
and Tim Rice and yielded, among other good songs, "Circle of Life."

☐ **MR. HOLLAND'S OPUS** (1995)
A stymied composer finds fulfillment as a high school English teacher in this
overly sentimental film that is more about music than it is a musical. The
soundtrack, however, runs the gamut from Gershwin to Beethoven, and is a
must-see for anyone thinking about a career in music.

☐ **SHINE** (1996) 🔲
Geoffrey Rush stars as Australian pianist David Helfgott, a child prodigy who
overcomes child abuse only to end up institutionalized. Years later he begins
playing in a piano bar before finally returning to the concert hall. Through
the course of the story a great deal of glorious music can be heard.

☐ **THAT THING YOU DO** (1996)
This fable about The Wonders, a rock band formed just after the Beatles
invaded America in 1964, is symbolic of the many wannabes and one-hit
wonders that followed the Fab Four. Tom Hanks stars, with lots of great

★BEST *of the* BEST★

☐ **EVITA** (1996)

By far the best film musical produced in the last two decades of the twentieth century, *Evita* was snubbed by a lot of critics who did not give Madonna the credit she deserves for her performance. Known for her cute but thin voice, Madonna took singing lessons to prepare for the role. They paid off; she is up to the task and really carries the movie. Unlike some revered film musicals of the past, this one uses the real voices of the actors, including Antonio Banderas and Jonathan Pryce. This is another fine example of a superb stage musical turned into a believable film through the use of realistic sets. You'll hardly notice that the entire story is told without the benefit of dialogue, with the exception of a few snippets. The subject matter alone is daring for a musical—namely, the rise to fame of Argentine fascist Juan Perón and his power-hungry wife Eva, or Evita, as she was called by those who adored her. While the entire score by Tim Rice and Andrew Lloyd Webber is brilliant, the most powerful songs are "Don't Cry for Me, Argentina," "I'd Be Surprisingly Good for You," and the Oscar-winning "You Must Love Me." Follow a viewing of this fictionalized account by reading about the real Eva Perón, and you will appreciate this achievement all the more. Jimmy Nail playing the lecherous worm Magaldi was a stroke of casting genius; watch and dislike him as he sings "On This Night of a Thousand Stars."

Jonathan Pryce and Madonna

supporting cast members, including Rita Wilson (Hanks's wife) and Chris Isaak. The soundtrack features a couple dozen songs, unfortunately not a hit among them.

☐ **ANASTASIA** (1997) 

Anastasia, murdered daughter of the last monarch of Imperial Russia, was rumored to have escaped execution, and several imposters during the twentieth century attempted to cash in on that rumor. This film plays with that story, while stressing the themes of family and home. You may recognize many of the voices in the beautiful score.

## ☐ HERCULES (1997)

Another animated Disney favorite, the great soundtrack and male hero make this mythological tale especially appealing to boys. The film tells the story of how Hercules, son of the Greek gods Zeus and Hera, is stripped of his immortality as an infant and must become a true hero in order to reclaim it.

## ☐ SELENA (1997)

Jennifer Lopez does an incredible job in this biopic about the murdered Latina singer Selena Quintanilla-Pérez. The voice you hear is that of the real Selena. Even though Lopez is a fine singer, the filmmakers felt that Selena's fans would not appreciate her songs being sung by another voice—a questionable decision, considering that it was the president of her fan club who murdered her. This is a sad story about success and celebrity. Don't miss it.

## ☐ WAITING FOR GUFFMAN (1997)

You have to see it for yourself to find out where you stand on this film, which is less a musical and more a, well, mocksical. It's the story of an aspiring

Christopher Guest in *Waiting for Guffman*

director, played by Eugene Levy, and the marginally talented amateur performers in the cast of a musical production being staged in a goofy small town in Missouri. When it's said that someone from Broadway will be in the audience, the troupe goes nuts. Also in the cast are Fred Willard, Christopher Guest, and the always hilarious Catherine O'Hara.

### ☐ DANCE WITH ME (1998)

Vanessa Williams stars in this romantic and underrated musical with scenes in Cuba and Florida that lend an authenticity and sincerity to the simple love story. Costar Chayanne and appearances by Kris Kristofferson, Joan Plowright, and Jane Krakowski (all dancing) make for many memorable moments as the young lovers-to-be strive for success in a dance contest. The perfect romantic Latin film, eternally optimistic, this movie is a keeper. Underlying the music is a serious story about immigration and Cuban-American relations. Williams doesn't sing, but the slow buildup to the dance numbers with Chayanne is sexy and beautiful, the best set featuring Cuban singer Albita.

### ☐ MULAN (1998) 🔅

In this Chinese fairy tale, a girl masquerades as a boy and delivers some good lessons on the concept of honor as she tries to save her disabled father. Boys may respond to this film better than to the standard Disney "princess" stories.

### ☐ JOSEPH AND THE AMAZING TECHNICOLOR DREAMCOAT (1999)

This film based on the popular stage play stars Donny Osmond, who is very funny in the role that made him even more adored than he was as the youngest of the singing Osmond brothers. Cleverly filmed as a classroom presentation with the students as the chorus, the biblically based story of attempted fratricide and the importance of hope and forgiveness is told entirely in music, with Maria Friedman as the narrator and Joan Collins as the greedy wife of the Potiphar, captain of the Egyptian palace guard. This is not the benign show it might appear to be at first, and it mixes up time and cultural references in dreamlike fashion. This Tim Rice and Andrew Lloyd Webber creation is not aimed at the wee ones; children are probably ready to see it about the time they are ready to learn how much violence and sex there really is in the Bible.

☐ **TARZAN** (1999) 🕷

This treatment of the Tarzan story really becomes a lesson on the way human beings treat the other animals that inhabit our planet. Most of the music, written by Phil Collins, is underscore, with the exception of "Trashin' the Camp" and "You'll Be in My Heart," making it perhaps a good choice for boys to start their musical education with.

# SOMETHING DIFFERENT

## Bizarre, Macabre, Retro

**AYBE NOT ENOUGH TIME HAS PASSED, BUT NO** musical of the twenty-first century yet ranks as an all-time-great film. There have been some interesting attempts to create a unique musical—*Moulin Rouge!* and *Hedwig and the Angry Inch* come to mind—but how many times we'll be watching them in the future remains to be seen.

The taste for such macabre fare as *Sweeney Todd: The Demon Barber of Fleet Street*, *Dancer in the Dark*, and *Repo! The Genetic Opera* is also bound to pass. The twenty-first century has seen a renewed interest in more traditional singing and dancing in feature films, yielding *Chicago*, *Mamma Mia!*, and *High School Musical*.

It seems fitting that this list of must-see musicals from their beginnings in 1927 should end in 2011 with a silent film, making a complete circle back to the dawn of the talkies. How a silent film can be a musical will become clear when you see *The Artist*.

☐ **ALMOST FAMOUS** (2000)
A high school boy gets a chance to write a story for *Rolling Stone* magazine about a rock band, and that means accompanying it on a concert tour. Kate Hudson gives a standout performance as a groupie, and some fifty songs by various music superstars—from Simon and Garfunkel to Alvin and the Chipmunks—make up the soundtrack.

☐ **DANCER IN THE DARK** (2000)
Alternately bewildering and compelling, this musical tragedy is played out ironically against an amateur production of *The Sound of Music*. An acting vehicle for the post–punk rock diva Björk, this film is grim. Brace yourself for her performance as a young Czech immigrant in Washington State in 1964 who is going blind and trying to find the money to save her ten-year-old son from the same fate. Occasionally she and other cast members burst into song—in a factory, on a train trestle, in prison—in this relentlessly bleak film. It's nice to see Joel Grey (of *Cabaret* fame) back on screen, singing and dancing to "In the Musicals." Catherine Deneuve (see her in *The Umbrellas of Cherbourg*) is also back as the sympathetic coworker and even sings and dances a bit. But this dark and emotionally draining tale is not for the children.

☐ **DUETS** (2000)
This amusing film about karaoke features Gwyneth Paltrow, Huey Lewis, and some of the great hits of the recent past. Maya Rudolph does "Hit Me with Your Best Shot," and Maria Bello sings the classic "I Can't Make You Love Me." Although largely panned by critics, the movie is worth watching for the music.

☐ **LOVE'S LABOUR'S LOST** (2000)
A contemporary musical version of the classic Shakespeare play directed by Kenneth Branagh, this movie is filmed as if it were a classic 1930s musical, so it's even more fun to watch after you've seen a few classic 1930s musicals. The soundtrack is loaded with songs by the great composers Cole Porter, George Gershwin, Jerome Kern, and Irving Berlin.

☐ **O BROTHER, WHERE ART THOU?** (2000)
This quirky comedy from the Coen brothers offers a unique opportunity to watch handsome and charming George Clooney behave like a goofball and

John Turturro, Tim Blake Nelson, and George Clooney in *O Brother, Where Art Thou?*

sing like a yokel. (Although he's dubbed, it's said he wanted to do his own singing and practiced hard for the part.) Clooney and his companions, having sprung from a chain gang in the Depression-era South, meet a motley cast of characters as they attempt to recover loot from a bank robbery. A series of strange encounters ensues, including the opportunity to make a record as the singing Soggy Bottom Boys. With some twenty songs scattered throughout this odyssey inspired by Homer, the film showcases bluegrass and country tunes authentic to the period, including "Po Lazarus," "You Are My Sunshine," "Down to the River to Pray," "I Am a Man of Constant Sorrow," and "I'll Fly Away."

## ☐ HEDWIG AND THE ANGRY INCH (2001)

John Cameron Mitchell stars in this unusual film about an angry transsexual performer whose sex-change operation has gone awry. If you can get past that premise, you might appreciate seeing a rock musical that isn't one hundred percent noise and mayhem, although the film just made me want to watch *The Sound of Music* one more time.

☐ **LAGAAN: ONCE UPON A TIME IN INDIA** (2001)

This list had to include at least one Bollywood film. I like this one a lot. The movie industry in India is producing countless musicals and light romances, but this one caught on quite a bit in the United States. The story about India under British rule is compelling; the lead actor, Aamir Khan, is handsome as all get out; and the music is joyous and may inspire you to check out more musicals from India.

☐ **MOULIN ROUGE!** (2001)

"The singing is okay, the spectacle is amazing," said *Broadway* magazine, and a bizarre and often boring spectacle it is. The spoof of *The Sound of Music* is apparent, but one does wonder why it is being done—half serious, half mockery, overlaid with absurdity. Prepare to have your senses assaulted and your musical assumptions challenged. You've got to know your musical history to appreciate the allusions in this satire. Incorporating a number of anachronistic songs and motifs, this odd spectacle ostensibly set in Paris in 1900 attempts to look at the mystique of the city and the Moulin Rouge nightclub from a new and surreal angle. The special effects are wonderful, but ultimately this film is more bizarre than engaging. If the credits had said, "Directed by Salvador Dalí," I would have believed them. If you have seen every film musical

Nicole Kidman and Ewan McGregor in *Moulin Rouge!*

made before this one, the echoes will resonate. Songs include "Nature Boy," "Lady Marmalade," and many other pop tunes.

## ☐ DRUMLINE (2002)

The basic story is of a band director who recruits a gifted Harlem street drummer to play in a Southern university marching band. The soundtrack is extensive, featuring numbers such as "Funky Drummer/Devon's Revenge." Young adults may find this especially appealing.

## ☐ 8 MILE (2002) 🔲

This semiautobiographical film stars Eminem as a Detroit rapper who very much resembles Eminem. That's on purpose, and there is an honesty and goodness in this movie that may take you by surprise. Everybody, including me, who has lived in Detroit any time since the 1960s recognizes the authenticity of this story and the cityscape against which it is told. Also, the soundtrack is a musical revelation.

## ☐ THE PIANIST (2002) 🔳

Not a musical by any stretch of the imagination, this film is one of Polish director Roman Polanski's crowning achievements. Adrien Brody stars as Polish-Jewish pianist Władysław Szpilman, dedicated to his art and a Holocaust survivor against all odds. The soundtrack is suitably Chopin, and the entire film is about dedication to music, to one's art above all.

## ☐ CAMP (2003)

Inspired by an actual summer camp for young actors, singers, and dancers, this dramatic and sometimes funny flick is a must see for young people dedicated to music and looking for a career. Critics found it unrealistic, but realism is seldom the best inspiration.

## ☐ CHICAGO (2003)

Employing every cliché ever uttered about Chicago and its 1920s gangster scene, *Chicago* nevertheless manages to be an entertaining musical—if you like your musicals mixed with murder and debauchery. Catherine Zeta-Jones really belts out "And All That Jazz," but the musical highlight for me has always been Queen Latifah singing "When You're Good to Mama" with lesbian inference. She's got the best voice in the film. "Cell Block Tango (He Had It

Coming)" and "All I Care About Is Love" are also showstoppers, and Richard Gere and Renée Zellweger pull off a couple of their best performances.

## ☐ A MIGHTY WIND (2003)

This subtle satire of folk music will not be to everyone's taste. As with all satire, the more you know about that which is being satirized, the more you'll get out of it. In this case, you might want to investigate the enormous appeal folk group Peter, Paul and Mary had in the 1960s. You'll see a lot of familiar comedic faces in this film, including Jane Lynch of *Glee* fame, but Catherine O'Hara and Eugene Levy carry the day with their mawkish portrayal of fictional folk legends Mitch and Mickey. Warning: This movie features a lot of talking, and if you don't get the joke, it's liable to bore you to tears.

## ☐ BEYOND THE SEA (2004)

Kevin Spacey stars in this underrated biopic about singer Bobby Darin. For some reason, critics didn't go crazy for this movie, but it really is something of a gem for the way it re-creates the 1960s. The movie spends a lot of time examining the relationship between Darin and his wife, Sandra Dee, but there is plenty of music in between the dramatic scenes, including one of Darin's biggest hits, "Mack the Knife." Spacey did his own singing for the film.

## ☐ DE-LOVELY (2004)

It may not be the greatest biopic ever made (the critics were brutal), and it may be too long or too slow in spots, but Kevin Kline is a pleasure to watch as he brings the life of Cole Porter to the screen again. (It was done in 1946 by Cary Grant in *Night and Day*.) One of the greatest American songwriters, Porter led a fascinating life but suffered greatly over his sexuality, despite his loving wife, played beautifully here by Ashley Judd. Over the course of the film you get to hear Porter's greatest hits, from "Night and Day" to "I Get a Kick Out of You."

## ☐ THE PHANTOM OF THE OPERA (2004)

Andrew Lloyd Webber's Broadway triumph made it to the screen after much delay and with the aid of a lot of technology and computer graphics. It's spectacular in many ways, and the music is gorgeous throughout. The sets are moody and sinister, the cinematography lavish. "Learn to Be Lonely," written for the film, was nominated for an Oscar for best song. Critics loved the art direction but felt less inclined to heap awards on the writing. Nevertheless,

Patrick Wilson and Emmy Rossum in *The Phantom of the Opera*

this is a beautiful and sophisticated film. The phantom's plight may strain your sympathy, especially once you've seen J. R. Martinez on *Dancing with the Stars*, but Minnie Driver brings welcome comic relief from the tedious love story.

## ☐ RAY (2004) 📷

Jamie Foxx shines in his Oscar-winning role as singer and pianist Ray Charles. Foxx actually seems to go blind in order to become Charles, as he delivers the story and the music with equal ability. Ray Charles himself is dubbed seamlessly for Foxx's voice, and we get to hear all the greatest hits without losing the tightly written story line. This is a musical not to be missed.

## ☐ SHALL WE DANCE (2004)

There's enough great music in this romantic comedy to call it a musical, and the dancing may have been the start of a trend that led to the appearance of *Dancing with the Stars* on television in 2005. Richard Gere plays a married man who becomes enchanted by a dancer, Jennifer Lopez, whom he sees from the window of the train he rides home from work. The dance scenes with Lopez exude the spice of life. The tango in the dark is so sexy, and the chemistry between Gere and Susan Sarandon, as his wife, would make any-body want to get married. This is a remake of a 1996 Japanese film of the same title that is well worth seeing.

☐ **CORPSE BRIDE** (2005) 🕷️
Also known as *Tim Burton's Corpse Bride*, this is the bizarre animated tale of a man and woman in a Victorian village who . . . well, you really have to see this to believe it. Burton's films are always strange and oddly good. This one boasts a superior soundtrack and many familiar voices bringing it to life, so to speak.

☐ **MRS. HENDERSON PRESENTS** (2005)
Another movie about the business of musical theater, this one puts an inter-esting spin on it, casting the great actress Judi Dench as an eccentric seventy-year-old widow who buys an old London theater and reopens it with a nude girlie review. The story is based on true events in the history of the Windmill Theater during World War II.

*Tim Burton's Corpse Bride*

☐ **THE PRODUCERS** (2005)

I've never been a big fan of this movie, even though most of my musical-loving friends find it falling-down-laughing funny, and it was a big hit on Broadway. Maybe I am just turned off by the whole premise, which is that a down-on-his-luck producer named Max Bialystock, played by Nathan Lane, teams up with a timid accountant, Leo Bloom, played by Matthew Broderick, in a get-rich-quick scheme to put on the world's worst show—a musical about Hitler and the Nazis. You should see this for the sheer outrageousness of it, but I don't think it's cute that the kids might walk away humming "Springtime for Hitler." The original (1968) version stars Zero Mostel and Gene Wilder.

☐ **RENT** (2005)

The film version of the award-winning Broadway musical about bohemians in New York's East Village is hampered by being almost ten years late in bringing their struggles with life, love, and AIDS to movie audiences. Nevertheless, the music is all there, including the beautiful "Seasons of Love." The Broadway show opened in 1996 and was marked by the sudden death of its creator, Jonathan Larson, the night before the off-Broadway premiere. The show won a Pulitzer Prize for Drama.

☐ **WALK THE LINE** (2005) 🎬

Joaquin Phoenix turns in a remarkable performance as country singer Johnny Cash, and in this biopic he actually does his own singing. The soundtrack is filled with great songs from the career of one of country-western's most versatile performers, who recorded alongside Elvis Presley, Jerry Lee Lewis, and Carl Perkins.

☐ **DREAMGIRLS** (2006) 🎬

Deny it as they may, the makers and stars of this film were at the very least inspired by the Supremes and the gripping story of the all-girl Motown trio's rise to international fame in the 1960s. Jamie Foxx, Beyoncé Knowles, Eddie Murphy, and Jennifer Hudson (who sings "And I Am Telling You I'm Not Going" in her Oscar-winning role) bring the story to life.

☐ **HIGH SCHOOL MUSICAL** (2006)

Leave it to the Disney Channel to tap into the enduring appeal of singing-and-dancing young people to create this enormously popular made-for-TV musical, which has spun off *High School Musical 2*, *High School Musical 3: Senior Year*, and a performance DVD called *High School Musical: The Concert*. The enormously wholesome and morally uplifting movies are a great antidote to the cynicism and anger that pervade so many contemporary films. On the other hand, the narcissism of these young folks puts *Fame* to shame, and after a while the concert begins to sound like a karaoke tape. I really prefer *Glee*.

□ **IDLEWILD** (2006)
Here's a film that doesn't know what it wants to be. Part of it is a brutal, graphic gangster movie and the other part a combination of *West Side Story* and Busby Berkeley. The setting is the American South during the Prohibition era; a speakeasy performer and club manager must fight off gangsters. More than two dozen songs make up the soundtrack, largely by the film's stars André Benjamin and Antwan A. Patton, aka André 3000 and Big Boi of the hip-hop duo OutKast, with perhaps the oddest number being "Chronomentrophobia" accompanied by cuckoo clocks. Others in the all-black cast include Terrence Howard, playing a convincing psychopath, and Paula Patton as the gorgeous and doomed singer Benjamin loves. The soundtrack is a creative anachronistic combination of big band, blues, and rap, but the musical numbers would make better music videos, especially with the dancers in the speakeasy. Make no mistake, this is a nasty movie, with the n-word and the f-word throughout, but it is an interesting experiment.

□ **A PRAIRIE HOME COMPANION** (2006)
Directed by the much-esteemed Robert Altman and written by the brilliant Garrison Keillor, this is a satirical look at what goes on backstage during the last broadcast of America's most celebrated radio show. If you love Keillor's radio show of the same title, be prepared for a disappointment. This is another film that is more concerned with what goes into making entertainment than in actually providing it. The immense talent of Meryl Streep and Lily Tomlin, playing a pair of gospel-singing sisters, is completely wasted, and it makes you wonder how a movie with this much going for it could be so boring.

□ **ACROSS THE UNIVERSE** (2007)
A romantic celebration of Beatles songs is deftly woven into the story of a young dockworker named Jude who leaves Liverpool to find his estranged father in America. Set in the late 1960s, this musical reinterprets those tur-

bulent times for a whole new generation through old song lyrics, as Jude falls in love with an American girl and they get caught up in the politics of a world gone psychedelic. A fine example of how the rock and roll canon can be kept alive through new ways of hearing it.

☐ **ENCHANTED** (2007)

I was enchanted by Disney's *Enchanted*, and I didn't expect to be. This has much to do with the performance of Amy Adams in what could have been a ridiculous role. Instead, she turns it into a very funny modern-day fairy tale in which an evil queen (Susan Sarandon) sends a storybook princess out to contend with a modern New York City, where she meets a handsome lawyer, played by Patrick Dempsey. Shades of Cinderella!

☐ **HAIRSPRAY** (2007)

It's impossible to take this movie too seriously, especially if you have seen *Grease* and realize that it's John Travolta playing Penny's big-hearted mother. This is a harmless mockery of the racism and conformity of the pre-sexual revolution 1960s, and everybody hams it up to tunes like "Good Morning Baltimore" and "Nicest Kids in Town." Queen Latifah gets in the act as Motormouth Maybelle, singing "Big, Blonde and Beautiful." Michelle Pfeiffer is hilarious as the bitchy stage manager singing "(The Legend of) Miss Baltimore Crabs." Nikki Blonsky stars as our heroine, the chubby girl with big hair and big dreams who delivers a rockin' stompin' good time for all. The film is a remake of the first and arguably better film version of *Hairspray* released in 1988 and starring Divine (once describved as the greatest drag queen of the twentieth century), Sonny Bono, Ruth Brown, Deborah Harry (lead singer of Blondie), and latter day talk show host Ricki Lake as the "pleasantly plump" Traci Turnblad. The memorable soundtrack of version one features music by Curtis Mayfield, Peggy March, Chubby Checker, Lesley Gore, Gene Pitney, and many other rock and roll icons.

☐ **LA VIE EN ROSE** (2007)

Marion Cotillard won a best actress Academy Award for her portrayal of "the Little Sparrow," Edith Piaf, whose dramatic rise to fame from poverty and poignant singing made her synonymous with Paris nightlife in the 1950s. Of course we get to hear the immortal title song, but also the equally compelling "Non, je ne regrette rien" in Piaf's own voice, in this superb biopic.

Susan Sarandon in *Romance and Cigarettes*

## ☐ ONCE (2007)

A delightful Irish film about a busker and an immigrant and their week in Dublin writing, rehearsing, and recording songs that will tell their love story. This surprising little gem pushes the boundaries of the musical genre in interesting ways. Definitely a musical to see after you've seen some much older ones. "Falling Slowly" is such a beautiful song.

## ☐ ROMANCE AND CIGARETTES (2007)

At last, a bitter film with a sweet center, in which a cheating husband (James Gandolfini, famous for his role in *The Sopranos*), an angry wife (Susan Sarandon of *The Rocky Horror Picture Show* and many other greater films), and their dysfunctional family in their bleak community sing their way through one of the most strangely touching films of the twenty-first century, with Kate Winslet delivering a poignant "other woman." Popular songs show up in utterly unexpected ways; among the most effective is Cyndi Lauper singing "Prisoner of Love." Although it is the exact opposite of glamorous, this film packs an emotional wallop very much like musicals from the golden age, and it redefines "happy ending." I'd have to watch this a few more times for a few more years before deciding it belongs in the pantheon of best musicals, but this brainchild of John Turturro is close already. Beware—critics disagree.

☐ **SWEENEY TODD: THE DEMON BARBER OF FLEET STREET** (2007)
Two things about this musical, successful as it may have been on Broadway, make it almost unwatchable for me. One: the topic—a vengeful man sets up a barbershop in London and ends up covering his murders by supplying meat for a pie store (if you get my drift). Two: although the film is based on the musical by the great Stephen Sondheim, it contains no memorable songs. Much as I love Johnny Depp—especially in *Edward Scissorhands*—this one is a must-see only if you love to hum "Springtime for Hitler" as you clear the dinner table.

☐ **CADILLAC RECORDS** (2008) 🎬
Beyoncé Knowles delivers a stunning performance as drug-addicted singer Etta James, while Adrien Brody stars as record mogul Leonard Chess in this tough story about the early days of crossover, when people like Chess, who founded Chess Records, had a difficult time selling authentic and talented black singers to white listening audiences. You get to hear Beyoncé reinterpret "At Last," which has to be one of the most enduring songs of the twentieth century, along with some great Chuck Berry songs as re-created by Mos Def, who plays Berry.

☐ **MAMMA MIA!** (2008)
A lot of people love to hate this musical, which is based on the totally singable, danceable music of the 1970s Swedish group ABBA. Meryl Streep is perhaps the most celebrated actress of her generation; when cast in this film she had already showed the world that she could do just about anything—except maybe sing. So here she comes, and not only can she sing, she becomes the life force that runs through this movie. The whole key to a performance like this is to look like you're having fun, but it takes a lot of planning to be spontaneous, and there's nothing about this seemingly effortless romp that isn't well choreographed and staged. You have to see this movie to understand how a series of good-natured pop tunes—"Dancing Queen," "Take a Chance on Me," "The Winner Takes It All," "Voulez Vous"—can be turned into movie magic.

☐ **REPO! THE GENETIC OPERA** (2008)
A desperately obvious attempt to create a cult classic, this one bases its draw on gore and the premise that in the not-so-distant future a worldwide epidemic of organ failures will devastate the world. A biotech company comes to the rescue, offering organ transplants at a price. Those who miss their pay-

ments, however, are scheduled for repossession. Paul Sorvino, Sarah Bright-
man, and Paris Hilton in the same movie—what more could a fan of the
macabre ask for? Personally, I would ask for *The Sound of Music*.

## ☐ THE ROCKER (2008)

It's difficult to make fun of something that's already as idiotic as heavy metal
and the rockers who play it in their egotistical glory. Heavy metal groups like
Kiss already seem to be making fun of themselves when they perform. So
what can a film like this add? Rainn Wilson is pretty funny as the man-child
loser who gets a second chance as a drummer, and Christina Applegate is very
convincing in her encouragement and support. In spite of the vulgarity and
having to be subjected to seeing Wilson naked, the story is rather sweet, and
the original songs and score by Chad Fischer do a good job of supporting it.

## ☐ HANNAH MONTANA: THE MOVIE (2009)

All that's required to love this movie is an appreciation for country music
(there is a hip-hop hoedown involved). This father-daughter story with Miley
Cyrus in her Montana persona and her real-life father Billy Ray Cyrus as her
father is probably better than you think, without taking itself too seriously.

## ☐ NINE (2009)

Worth watching for the virtuoso performances of Daniel Day-Lewis, Sophia
Loren, Judi Dench, Nicole Kidman, and others, this musical about an egotistical Italian man-child director never really takes off and never offers up
a truly memorable tune, with the possible exception of "My Husband Makes
Movies," sung by Marion Cotillard as the director's long-suffering wife.

## ☐ THE PRINCESS AND THE FROG (2009) 🕷

Tiana, Disney's first African American princess, is introduced in this film,
with music by the great Randy Newman. The soundtrack features jazz,
zydeco, blues, and gospel—authentic American musical styles. This is likely
to appeal to the adults in your household as well as the children.

## ☐ BURLESQUE (2010)

What sticks with you from this movie is what a good singer Christina Aguilera
really is. She polishes off "Diamonds Are a Girl's Best Friend" in a better voice

than Marilyn Monroe. The plot of the film is cliché-ridden, and no one who really performed in burlesque would recognize any of this as burlesque. But that is not the point. The reason to see this is to get a glimpse of what makes Aguilera so popular and to see how Cher's latest plastic surgery is holding up. As a story, it is predictable, but it takes some effort to produce so old-fashioned a musical in the twenty-first century, and Cher fans (of which I am one) will adore her singing "You Haven't Seen the Last of Me."

## ☐ TANGLED (2010)

This Disney creation features the magically long-haired Rapunzel, who has spent her life in a tower but is about to discover the world—and herself. The strong "prince" character is not a prince at all, and Rapunzel, while a princess, is more independent that many early Disney princesses. This story is likely to appeal to boys as well as girls.

## ☐ THE MUPPETS (2011)

The plot in a nutshell: With the help of three fans (Jason Segel, Amy Adams, and the voice of Peter Linz), the Muppets must reunite to save their old theater from a greedy oil tycoon, played by Chris Cooper. Destined to be an enduring favorite, this fabulous family fare garnered the Muppets their first Oscar, awarded to Bret McKenzie for best original song, "Man or Muppet." The music in this film is indeed enchanting and includes the old favorite "Rainbow Connection," as well as some familiar tunes like "Me and Julio Down by the Schoolyard," by Paul Simon, and "We Built This City," performed by Starship. "Life's a Happy Song" is the grand finale, performed by the whole gang.

## ☐ RIO (2011)

When a domesticated macaw from a small town in Minnesota meets the bird of his dreams, they take off on an adventure that takes them to Rio de Janeiro. The music of the great Sergio Mendes and other Latin American artists provides a delightfully danceable score in samba rhythms.

## ☐ WINNIE THE POOH (2011)

The classic tale by A. A. Milne gets a new musical treatment in this Disney creation that combines various adventures from the books. This is a gentle tale suitable for young children.

Jean Dujardin and Bérénice Bejo in *The Artist*

## ☐ THE ARTIST (2011)

It's fitting that this list end where it began, with a movie set in 1927, when the advent of "talkies" ended the career of many an actor and actress. *The Artist* is a little French film that took the world by storm, even though it is a black-and-white silent movie. How can a silent movie be a musical, you ask? Don't miss seeing this film and finding out for yourself. The performances of Jean Dujardin and Bérénice Bejo are musical throughout the film in many ways, and the closing dance number tells more about the transition from silent to sound than Al Jolson did more than eight decades ago.

# LEARN MORE

## RECOMMENDED READING, VIEWING, AND WEBSITES

**RECOMMENDED READING**

*The American Songbook: The Singers, the Songwriters, and the Songs,* by Ken Bloom, foreword by Michael Feinstein, New York, Black Dog and Leventhal Publishers, 2005. Generously illustrated history incorporating one hundred years of American popular music.

*Gotta Sing Gotta Dance: A Pictorial History of Film Musicals,* by John Kobal, London/New York/Sydney/Toronto, Hamlyn Publishing Group Ltd., 1971. Smart analysis of film musicals from the beginning through the 1960s.

*The Great Movie Musical Trivia Book,* by Jeff Kurtti, introduction by Shirley Jones, New York, Applause Books, 1996. A wealth of tidbits about the author's top ten: *The Wizard of Oz, Singin' in the Rain, Guys and Dolls, My Fair Lady, Mary Poppins, Willy Wonka and the Chocolate Factory, The Music Man, Hello, Dolly!, Snow White and the Seven Dwarfs,* and *Beauty and the Beast.*

*The Hollywood Musical,* by Ethan Mordden, New York, St. Martin's Press, 1981. This is a blessedly frank and witty assessment of musicals—their stars, directors, and writers—with an entertaining "Hall of Fame and Disrepute" addendum.

*Hollywood Musicals: The 101 Greatest Song-and-Dance Movies of All Time,* by Ken Bloom, foreword by Jane Powell, New York, Black Dog and Leventhal Publishers, 2010. This beautifully illustrated, colorful coffee-table book also includes sections on the treatment of women and men in musicals, foreign musicals, great numbers from musicals, black musicals, Jewish musicals, and the worst movie musicals.

*Hollywood Musicals: Year by Year*, by Stanley Green, revised and updated by Barry Monush, third edition, New York, Applause Theatre and Cinema Books, 2010. Chronological, selective listings with complete production details, cast members, song lists, and illuminating histories of each film.

*The MGM Story: All 1,723 Films of MGM Described and Illustrated in Color and Black-and-White*, by John Douglas Eames, revised edition, New York, Crown Publishers, 1979. The annual output from 1924 to 1978, with a special section on Metro Goldwyn Mayer's great musicals.

*The Melody Lingers On: The Great Songwriters and Their Movie Musicals*, by Roy Hemming, New York, Newmarket Press, 1986. A thorough listing and analysis of the major creative forces behind the music and lyrics of musical films.

*Musicals! A Complete Selection Guide for Local Productions*, by Richard Chigley Lynch, second edition, Chicago and London, American Library Association, 1994. The classics and all the basics needed to make choices for putting on your own show.

*Popcorn: Fifty Years of Rock 'n' Roll Movies*, by Garry Mulholland, London, Orion Books Ltd., 2010. Readable analysis of how rock music and musicians have been portrayed in more than a hundred films, from *Jailhouse Rock* to *Hedwig and the Angry Inch*.

*The Sound of Music Family Scrapbook: The Inside Story of the Beloved Musical, Revealed by the Actors Who Starred as the von Trapp Children*, by Fred Bronson, with Charmian Carr, Nicholas Hammond, Heather Menzies, Duane Chase, Angela Cartwright, Debbie Turner, and Kym Karath, Montclair, New Jersey, Applause Theatre and Cinema Books, 2012. If you are a fan, this is a beautiful, delightful must.

## RECOMMENDED VIEWING

*The Great American Songbook: Celebrating 100 Years of Music in America*, Warner Home Video, 2003. Hosted by Michael Feinstein, this musical history is filled with clips and rare footage of the best American music makers. An excellent introduction to the canon.

*Hollywood Singing and Dancing: The Series, 1920s thru the 2000s*, Great Musical Treasures, 2008–2010. A thirteen-part series exploring the grandest musicals that Hollywood has ever produced. Hosted by Oscar winner Shirley Jones, this is a celebration of song and dance, from the Busby Berkeley era to more recent smash hits like *Dreamgirls* and *Hairspray*.

*MGM, When the Lion Roars: The Story of a Hollywood Empire*, Warner Home Video, 1992, 2009 on DVD. This story of the film studio that made the most lavish and enduring musicals is told with plenty of clips from the best of the lot. Another great tool for choosing what to see in full.

*That's Entertainment! The Complete Collection (That's Entertainment; That's Entertainment, Part 2*; and *That's Entertainment III)*, Warner Home Video, 2004. This four-disc boxed set is a great introduction to film musicals, a revelation to me because it showed me how many musicals I had never seen. Take notes as you watch!

*WWII, the Music Video: The Songs We Sang, the Stars We Loved*, Universal Archives Congress Video Group, volume 1, 1989, and volume 2, 1991. I can't resist including these, two of my favorite old VHS tapes, because they include such great samples of the music of the 1940s, the music that inspired "the greatest generation" as they fought and won World War II. They are hard to find, but ask for them, anyway!

## RECOMMENDED WEBSITES

AMC Filmsite. www.filmsite.org/musicalfilms.html

Amazon.com. www.amazon.com. Build your own library.

EW: Entertainment Weekly. "25 Greatest Movie Musicals of All Time!" www.ew.com/ew/gallery/0,,20164491,00.html#20377168

Facets Multimedia: Your Source for World Cinema. www.facetsmovies.com/user/movieBrowseByType.php

Metacritic: Keeping Score of Entertainment. www.metacritic.com

Michael Feinstein's American Songbook. www.michaelfeinsteinsamerican songbook.org

Moviefone: Best Movie Musicals of All Time. http://blog.moviefone.com/ 2009/12/16/best-movie-musicals

Internet Movie Database. www.imdb.com/genre/musical

Library of Congress: National Film Registry and National Film Preservation Board. www.loc.gov/film

ScreenCrave. http://screencrave.com/2008-11-17/top-10-movie-musicals-of -all-time

# INDEX